WOMEN EMPOWERMENT AND LEADERSHIP

DR SAVITA MISHRA

Made with ♥ on the Notion Press Platform
www.notionpress.com

Contents

Preface

Women's education is crucial to growth and development of a country. No country can sustainably develop economically without significant investments in female education. As mentioned by Desmond Tutu, ***"If we are going to see real development in the world then our best investment is WOMEN!"***Through education, people gain a better understanding of themselves and the world around them. As a result, it improves the quality of their lives and benefits society at large. In addition to encouraging growth and creativity, women's education contributes to entrepreneurship and technical advancements. Furthermore, it plays a crucial role in economic and social development as well as in income distribution. There is a strong positive correlation between the education of women and the economic development of nations. Therefore, keeping in mind that women education is of great importance for the political and economic development of a nation, women's education has been a major concern of the government as well as civil society in India.

In a country like ours, women's education plays a crucial role in the whole development process. Women are more productive and families are more satisfied when they have higher literacy rates and educational levels. Increasing the education levels and literacy rates of women is one of the most effective investments for women. Well-educated women provide the skills, knowledge, and self-confidence that contribute to their success as a mother, a worker, and a citizen. The skills of an educated woman will also benefit her at work in terms of productivity and earnings. For women, the return on investment in education is often higher than for men. The reduction of gender inequality in literacy and primary, secondary, and management education is crucial to reducing poverty and accelerating sustainable development in developing countries. There is a gender gap in education, which is more pronounced in restricted areas. Education disparities are greater in educationally backward, traditionally captured regions and regions with low levels of development. Educated women are particularly skilled at developing plans for human habitat expansion.

At present, it is widely recognized that women play a crucial role in the economic development of a nation. A deeply entrenched patriarchal system heavily influenced their existence, with the result that their basic rights were often denied to them the same as those enjoyed by their male counterparts, including their right to education. Nevertheless, as legislation, social reforms, and women's movements arose worldwide, there was a major shift in the socio-cultural set up, and women's rights to education became increasingly recognized as critical for a nation's development. When women are denied an education, individuals, families, and children, as well as the societies in which they live, suffer. Educating women benefits everyone. Napoleon once said, ***"Give me an educated mother and I will give you a civilized, educated nation."*** Yet, we still have a long way to go before women around the world fulfill their educational potential for the good of society. Therefore, why do women in many developing countries continue to lag behind men in measures of educational attainment, including literacy, length of education, and educational attainment? This book will address those issues related to different opportunities and challenges of Women Education and further examine how educational decisions are made. This enriched volume illustrates the importance of women education and discusses its impact on the development of the nation which may hopefully be useful for the research scholars, academicians and prospective readers of Social Sciences.

The accomplishment of this work was possible with the blessing of our parents and family members who continuously inspired and guided us throughout this journey. We extend our sincere thanks to all the eminent contributors who have enriched this book with their provocative and diverse scholarly contributions. We would like to express our special thanks to the publishing house for their benevolent effort to give this book a finite form within the stipulated time.

Dr. Savita Mishra

CHAPTER ONE

Women Rights as Human Rights

Dr. S. K. Chaturvedi: Assistant Professor, Department of Law, H.N.B.Garhwal University (A Central University), SRT Campus, Tehri, Uttarakhand &

Shradha Baranwal: Assistant Professor, School of Law, University of Petroleum & Energy Studies, Dehradun, Uttarakhand

Abstract

Life, liberty, equality and dignity are the essential tenets of human rights. Human rights are also known as the natural rights, basic rights and common rights. The constitution of India also ensures the equality of rights of men and women. However, inside the sphere of women human rights in India, there exists a good wide hole between idea and practice. Women play a pivotal role within the development of any country. As per Article 15 of the Indian constitution, discrimination can't be made among citizens on the grounds of faith, religion, race, caste or sex. We see that each day and everywhere newspaper news, T V channels and Electronic devices are presenting to the violation of Human Rights of Women in India. Majority of the people presume that our society is a male ruled society wherein guys are continually assumed to be superior to society. The Indian women need to face to discrimination, injustice and dishonor. Although women in India have been given more rights in comparison to guys, even then the circumstance of girls in India is depressing. This paper argues that in India, women's rights are violated frequently in day-to-day life, within in the family, in households and within the property right. In a patriarchal society, women often suffer in silence, deprived of personal liberty and bound by rules made by the allegedly superior males.

Key –words- Human rights, fundamental rights, Article15, women's rights, personal liberty

"Freedom means the supremacy of human rights everywhere. Our support goes to those who struggle to gain those rights and keep them. Our strength is our unity of purpose. To that high concept, there can be no end save victory." — **Franklin D. Roosevelt**

Introduction

In ancient India, women were revered and considered significant considering the welfare of the family and society. The women were given a high status within society, and they felt gratified and contented. They were provided with the opportunity to attain high intellectual and spiritual standards .Women's rights activists mobilized to ensure that woman's human rights were fully on the agenda of the international community under the rallying cry "Women's Rights are Human Rights."The slogan 'Women's Rights are Human rights' was first used at the UN World Conference on human rights in Vienna in 1993. This slogan signifies, firstly, that women as a class have been denied fundamental human rights for centuries and have been subject to the worst forms of bigotry, discrimination, and exploitation. On the other hand, it means that actual support of human rights is not possible unless the exponent also vows to support and uphold rights that are available only to women like equality with men, maternal health and sexual and reproductive rights, freedom from gender-based violence, and high-quality education.

In 1948, the Universal Declaration of Human Rights was adopted. It, too, proclaimed the equal entitlements of women and men to the rights contained in it, "without distinction of any kind, such as ... sex," In drafting the Declaration, there was considerable discussion about the use of the term "all men" rather than a gender-neutral term. The Declaration was eventually adopted using the terms "all human beings" and "everyone" to leave no doubt that the Universal Declaration was intended for everyone, men and women alike.

What are human rights?

Human rights are natural rights, basic rights which should be enjoyed by all people in society. Human beings should have rights that help them to live good, comfortable, and meaningful life. The right to live with human dignity and freedom is a God-given gift to every person born in this world. The great challenge of this paper is to recognize the importance of women's rights and give voice to women everywhere whose experiences go unnoticed, whose words go unheard so that this effort may strengthen families and societies by empowering women to take greater control over their own destinies.

According to Section 2(d) of the Human Rights Protection Act, 1993, "Human rights" means the rights relating to life, liberty, equality, and dignity of the individual guaranteed by the Constitution or embodied in the International Covenants and enforceable courts in India. Human rights are rights granted to us merely because we exist as humans. These are independent of, for example, gender, nationality, skin color or religion. In other words, they are universal: they apply to all people. These human rights range from a fundamental right to life to the rights to food, health, work, education, and liberty.

Human rights and fundamental freedoms should be birthrights, but across the globe, some countries fail to accord human rights to women. Moreover, women are often victims of human rights abuses. Women's human rights are abused when they cannot participate in decisions that affect their lives and are denied political participation and fair representation when they are prevented from going to school or receiving health care, when they face discrimination in employment, when they are denied equal rights to own land and property, when they suffer from violence within their homes and when they are subjected to harmful traditional practices such as genital mutilation and honor killings.

An International Women's Bill of Rights

The Convention on the Elimination of All Forms of Discrimination Against Women (CEDAW), a key international agreement on women's human rights, was adopted by the United Nations General Assembly in 1979. It is often described as an international bill of rights for women. Its preamble and 30 articles aim to eliminate gender discrimination and promote gender equality. The convention defines discrimination against women as "any distinction, exclusion or restriction made on the basis of sex" that impedes women's "human rights and fundamental freedoms in the political, economic, social, cultural, civil or any other field." It sets an agenda for national action to end such discrimination, requiring all parties to the convention to take "all appropriate measures, including legislation, to ensure the full development and advancement of women" and guarantee their fundamental freedoms "on a basis of equality with men."

As of 2021, 189 United Nations member states had ratified CEDAW. The Obama administration strongly supports this treaty and is committed to U.S. ratification. State parties to CEDAW agree to incorporate principles of gender equality into their national constitutions or other appropriate legislation; to adopt appropriate legislation and other measures that prohibit discrimination against women; and to establish legal protections of their rights on an equal basis with men.

Women's human rights apply to both the "public" and "private" spheres of women's lives. For many governments, however, addressing women's rights in the "private" sphere is challenging because the private sphere is often thought to be beyond the purview of the state, exempt from governmental scrutiny and intervention .As a result, in many countries, discrimination and violence against women and girls occur in the family and under the guise of religious and cultural traditions. Its practices continue to remain hidden in the private sphere, where perpetrators of such human rights abuses typically enjoy impunity for their actions.

Origin and Development of Women's Rights

Human rights discourse had traditionally been male-dominated in the sense that, in what is essentially a man's world, men have struggled to assert their dignity and common humanity against an overbearing state apparatus.

Attempts to define a body of civil and political thoughts were made from the eighteenth century onwards in societies that were organized by men and, predominantly for men. Plato was the first Greek political philosopher who tried to emancipate women from their household duties of childbearing and rearing so that they can contribute equally to state affairs. Therefore, he gave the theory of communism of wives to the guardian class. Since ancient times, so many philosophers have talked about the rights of women and natural rights worldwide. Likewise, Ancient Greek philosophers followed the universalism of law by equality in various aspects of life, "equal respect for all citizens, equality before the law, equality in political power and suffrage, and equality of civil rights." Women played an insignificant role in the determination of political, legal, and institutional structures both in the USA and in Europe where much of the human rights debate was perused. The original contributors to women's human rights were those who first taught women to read and thus explore the world outside the home and immediate community. Lone voices, such as that of Mary Wollstonecraft, did attempt to vindicate the right of women and a certain philosophical tradition did develop in which pleas were made for the emancipation of women to allow them to escape their traditional domestic role and to enter more fully in into society.

Women's Rights as Human Rights

Since the 1980s, women around the world have come together in networks and coalitions to raise awareness about problems of discrimination, inequality, and violence. They have used a human rights framework to fight for women's rights in the family, social, economic, and political arenas. An important outcome of the 1995 Beijing Fourth World Conference on Women was the Beijing Declaration and Platform for Action. These documents embody the international community's commitment to advance and empower women and remove obstacles in the public and private spheres that have historically limited women's full participation. The Platform for Action sets forth three strategic objectives related to the human rights of women: to promote and protect women's human rights through the full implementation of all human rights instruments (especially CEDAW), to ensure equality and nondiscrimination under the law and in practice, and to achieve legal literacy. Governments bear the main responsibility, but persons, organizations and enterprises are important in taking concrete actions to improve women's lives.

Then-U.S. first lady Hillary Clinton famously declared at the 1995 Beijing conference that "human rights are women's rights," adding, "Women must enjoy the right to participate fully in the social and political lives of their countries if we want freedom and democracy to thrive and endure."

The CEDAW, adopted by the UN General Assembly on December 18, 1979, gives all member states a template to eliminate all forms of discrimination against women. India ratified CEDAW in 1993.CEDAW and the Beijing Declaration and Platform for Action signaled the successful mainstreaming of women's rights as human rights. Although the Beijing Declaration and Platform for Action are not legally binding, they do carry ethical and political weight and can be used to pursue local, regional, and national efforts to address women's human rights. CEDAW is a treaty that is binding on its parties.

The principles and practices related to women's human rights are continuously evolving. The large body of international covenants, agreements, and commitments to women's human rights developed over the past several decades provides women with an alternative vision and vocabulary to confront violations to their human rights. Such guidelines are important tools for political activism and a framework for developing concrete strategies for change.

WOMEN'S HUMAN RIGHTS IN INDIA

The Indian Constitution Should provide and Guarantee the Human Rights for women to live best with dignity in society. These are -

- Right to equality
- Right to education
- Right to live with dignity
- Right to liberty
- Right to politicsv Right to property
- Right to equal opportunity for employment
- Right to free choice of profession
- Right to livelihood
- Right to work in equitable condition Right to get equal wages for equal work
- Right to protection from gender discrimination

- Right to social protection in the eventuality of retirement, old age, and sickness
- Right to protection from inhuman treatment
- Right to protection of health
- Right to privacy in terms of personal life, family, residence, correspondence, etc. and

VIOLATION OF WOMEN HUMAN RIGHTS IN INDIA:

It is claimed that Indian women have been given the equal rights as their male counterparts and there is no discrimination on the basis of sex, but the actual condition of the Indian women cannot be said satisfactory. There exists a huge gap between de facto and de jure condition due to the present structure of Indian society and practices prevalent in it. India has a patriarchal society where male dominates and always are treated as superior in compare to their female counterparts, that is why the condition of Indian women is not as good as men's

After 75years of Independence, India continues to have significant human rights problems despite making commitments to tackle some of the most prevalent abuses. On paper, women have been given ample rights but in practice, the women in India have been the sufferers from the past and even today also, they have to face discrimination, injustice, and dishonor. Let us now discuss the crimes done against women despite being given rights equal to men. These points will explain the continuous violation of the human rights of women in India. Even though strong laws at the national level, women and girls across India continue to suffer routine domestic violence, acid attacks, rape, and murder. The government has failed to hold public officials accountable when they fail to enforce policies designed to protect women and children.

VIOLATION OF RIGHTS FROM SOCIETY, STATE AND FAMILY SYSTEM:

1) CHILD MARRIAGES:

Child marriage is most prominent area in violation of rights from society. It has been traditionally prevalent in India and continues to this date. According to the law, a girl cannot be married until she has reached the age of 18 at least. But the girl in India is still taken as a burden on the family. Sometimes the marriages are settled even before the birth of the child. Parents also believe that it is easy for the child–bride to adapt to the new environment as well as it is easy for others to mold the child to suit their family environment. Some believe that they marry girls at an early age to avoid the risk of their unmarried daughters getting pregnant. This shows that the reasons for child marriages in India are so baseless. Basically, this phenomenon of child marriage is linked to poverty, illiteracy, dowry, landlessness, and other social evils. The impact of child marriage is widowhood, inadequate socialization, education deprivation and lack of independence to select a life partner, lack of economic independence, and low nutritional levels because of early pregnancies in an unprepared psychological state of a young bride. The child marriage also affects health issue. Although, legislations for child marriage prohibition has been passed by Parliament, nevertheless cases relating to child marriages is still increasing specially in rural sectors. Many people are not well aware about the legislation pertaining to child marriages. So, all this indicated that immediate steps should be taken to stop the evil of Child Marriage.

2) DOWRY HARASSMENT AND BRIDE BURNING: Indian society has been stigmatized by many social and legal problems. One of such major problem is the dowry system that still prevails in the society. Though such practice is condemned by law still it is a custom that is performed in various parts of India. The demands for dowry by the husband and his family and then the killing of the bride because of not bringing enough dowries to the in-laws have become a very common crime these days. Despite the legislation on dowry has been passed by the government, which has made dowry demands in weddings illegal, the dowry incidents are increasing day by day.

3) RAPE: Rape, the English word is derived from Latin word *rapere*. According to the Merriam Webster dictionary rape is an 'unlawful sexual activity.' Rape is one of the India's most common crimes committed against women. Young girls in India often are the victims of rape. Almost 255 rapes are of girls under 16 years of age. The law against rape is unchanged for 120 years. In rape cases, it is torturous for the victim to prove that she has been raped. The victim finds it difficult to undergo a medical examination immediately after the trauma of the assault. Besides this, the family too is reluctant to bring in prosecution due to family prestige and hard police procedures.

4) DOMESTIC VIOLENCE: The 'World Human Rights Conference in Vienna' first recognized gender-based violence as a human rights violation in 1993. Wife beating and abuses by alcoholic husbands are violence done against women which are never publicly acknowledged. The cause is mainly the man demanding the hard-earned money of his wife for his drinking. But Indian woman always tries to conceal it as they are ashamed of talking about it. In most cases, women are unwilling to go to court because of a lack of an alternative support system. But, the situation has been changed. The awareness has come both in rural as well as in urban sectors. Women's are visiting courts for their rights.

CONCLUSION:

Human rights are those minimum rights that are compulsorily accessible by every individual as she is a member of the human family. The constitution of India also guarantees the equality of rights of men and women. The government(Central, State, and local) will provide all types of security for violated women in society and take needful action to not violate their rights. And all are given to respect women in our society by human nature to support them and encourage for freely independent living in our society. Women's rights and equity must be looked at with renewed vigor and vision. It should be an integral part of the development and welfare policies of states and international organizations. Awareness campaigns should be organized on women's rights by civil society and freedoms and disseminate knowledge of the various welfare measures implemented by the state and international organizations. We also must recognize that women will never gain full dignity until their human rights are respected and protected.

References:

1. Paylee, M.V. Constitutional Government in India, Rev. edition, 6, S. Chand & Company Ltd., New Delhi, 2006.
2. Ahuja Ram, Violence against Women, Rawat Publication, Jaipur, 1998
3. Shukla V.N , The Constitution of India, EBC, 13th Edition 2017
4. The Human Rights Protection Act, 1993
5. The Universal Declaration Of Human Rights 1948
6. Kapoor S. K., Human Rights, Central Law Agency, Allahabad, 5th Edition, 2011.

CHAPTER TWO

Education and Empowerment of Women Through Inclusive Policies

Dr. Tulika Chakravorty:Assistant Professor, Bangabasi Morning College, Kolkata

The best thermometer to the progress of a nation is its treatment of its women. The great Aryans, Buddha among the rest, have always put woman in an equal position with man. For them sex in religion did not exist. In the Vedas and Upanishads, women taught the highest truths and received the same veneration as men. – Swami Vivekananda

Abstract

The broad objective of the development programme is to improve the quality of life of the people. But the development can only be sustained when the people will build their own capacity to solve the problems and take decision in the management of their own resources. Education and only education is the parameter which can lead a society towards development. The present article focuses on the National inclusive policies implemented for the promotion of education level of the women for the growth of the nation.

Key words: Women's Education, Capacity Building, Empowerment, Inclusive Policies

Introduction

The Belief that women have to depend on men to be great is a myth, and that such a belief is a myth is proved by the blazing life-stories of great women. For Swami Vivekananda women were the condensed forms of all powerful Feminine (Shakti). In his view the only thing needed was to awaken this awareness in the women folk, and the rest would be easy. By true education of the women strong character is formed, strength of mind is increased, the intellect is expanded and by which one can stand on one's feet. Swamiji believed that with such an education women will be capable to solve their own problems.

Empowerment can be understood by "recognizing the capacities of such groups (the marginalized and oppressed) to take action and to play an active role in development initiatives". Oakley identifies five key uses of the term empowerment in development studies. These are: empowerment as participation, empowerment as democratization, empowerment as capacity building, empowerment as capacity building, empowerment through economic improvement and empowerment at the individual level.

Naila Kabeer refers empowerment as the "process by which those who have been denied the ability to make strategic life choices acquire such ability". This definition makes clear that only those previously denied such abilities can be considered to be empowered and also that the choices in question are strategic. Kabeer defines strategic choices as ones "which are critical for people to live the lives they want (such as choice of livelihood, whether and who to marry, whether to have children etc)" as opposed to "less consequential choices which may be important for the quality of one's life but do not constitute its defining parameters".

Naila Kabeer (1994) subscribes not so much to 'power over' but to 'power within' that needs to be strengthened; power within needs recognition by experience and analysis of the subordination of women. According to Kabeer, such power cannot be given; it has to be self – generated and taken. Empowerment is a process where women are able to change from a state of powerlessness ('I cannot') to a state of collective self – confidence ('we can').Development of women, safeguarding their interest is to ensure that they are brought into the mainstream to take advantage of the general development activities. The various efforts and activities for the development of women are based on the empowerment strategy and policy making.

Inclusive Policies for improving the Education level of Women:

Education, especially women's education, is generally considered a key factor to development. It is related to demographic parameters and other indicators of health and socio – economic conditions of a population, or a nation as a whole. It not only helps in the development of half of the human resources, but in improving the quality of life at home and outside. Educated women not only tend to promote education of their girl education, but also can provide better guidance to all their children. Moreover, educated women can also help in the reduction of infant mortality rate and growth of the population. Moreover, maternal education is related to child health because it reduces the cost of public health programmes relating to information on health technology, increases household income and productivity of health inputs. So it is necessary to increase in investment in formal education of female, for the best health development agenda.

An International Conference on Population and Development (ICPD) in Cairo, held in 1994, has strongly recommended that all countries should take immediate steps to achieve the goal of universal primary education before the year 2015, and to ensure that girls and women should get the widest and earliest possible access to secondary and higher levels of education.

It is envisaged that only education empowering poor backward women and thus they will be able to participate fully in social, economic and political process, which affect their lives and be able to take control of them.

According to the World Population Report (1990), 'A mother's education is the single most important factor in keeping her family small and her children alive. Education is the first line of defense for women faced with the lifethreatening situation that traditional life styles perpetuate. It encourages the sense of control over personal destiny. It opens the door to choices that are not beyond bound by tradition. With an education, the women's status steps beyond the confines of motherhood. Further, the quality of life in the family of educated women becomes a priority'.

The Government of India for the first time accepted the concept of 'investment' in education in its 1968 Policy and quantitatively fixed a target of six percent of national income to be invested on education from the public exchequer by 1986. Some efforts have been initiated in recent years towards mobilization of non – governmental resources, mainly for secondary and higher education. The measures include introduction of cost recovery measures, introduction and revitalization of student loan programmes in higher education, and mobilization of community resources for primary education. These are in addition to measures being taken towards privatization of education and thus again marginalized sections of the society are lagging behind in the process of development through education.

Though several measures were being taken for improving the education level of women; still the country yet to realize its goal in this section. Some of the measures are:

Education Guarantee Scheme (EGS):

A novel scheme called Education Guarantee Scheme has been viewed as an effective answer to the problem of physical access to schools. This is an important initiative that the government has taken at the national level in 1999 – 2000. The purpose of this programme was to provide an opportunity to the rural poor, especially those belonging to the Scheduled Castes, Scheduled Tribes and other backward classes to secure education for their children. The scheme is meant for those areas where no school currently exists within a radius of 1 km. These areas could be the areas where the poorest of the poor live. The EGS envisages the poor local community to a) come forward, expressing demand for a school, b) specifically provide the premises required for a school, c) provide for a local part time teacher and d) maintain the school at least for two years with the gram panchayat mobilizing contributions in cash and kind from the local community. Now it has been made a part of the Sarva Shiksha Abhiyaan.

Operation Blackboard:

The government of India has initiated the Operation Blackboard programme, as a follow – up of the National Policy on Education 1986 to improve the infrastructure facilities, and quality of primary education. The scheme was started in 1987 – 88 and aimed at substantial improvement in basic facilities in all primary schools run by government and local bodies. It consists of three different components: a) a building comprising at least two reasonably large all weather rooms with a deep verandah and separate toilet facilities for boys and girls, b) at least two teachers in every school, as far as possible one of them a woman and a third teacher if the enrolment in a school is above 100, and c) essential teaching learning material including blackboards, maps, charts, toys and equipment for work experience including teacher's material and miscellaneous facilities (water facilities), etc. The Revised National Policy on Education (1992) suggested an expansion of the scope of Operation Blackboard to provide three reasonably large rooms and three teachers in every primary school, and to extend the scheme to upper primary level.

Free Elementary Education:

To reduce the households direct costs of schooling of children, like many other countries had resolved long ago to provide free elementary education- specifically tuition fee free. The Government of India has also recommended in the Programme of Action, expansion of the existing schemes more intensively to the target population groups. For example, it suggested the provision of two sets of free uniforms, free text books and stationary, and attendance incentives to the girls of all families below the poverty line, and provision of free transport in state roadways buses and local trains to children attending elementary schools, etc. In fact, the Government of India has promised, in the Programme of Action, that 'a comprehensive system of incentives and support services will be provided for girls and children of the economically weaker sections of society'.

Decentralization of Education:

An important development of the 1990s refers to significant efforts of the government to decentralize educational planning and administration and the involvement of the community at various levels(like School Committee, Panchayat Education Committee, Municipal Education Committee, District Education Committee with two boards, one at the district level called District Education Board and state level board called State Advisory Board for School Education) in planning, administration, financing, monitoring, and supervision of the working of the school system. Following the Constitutional Amendment in favour of Panchayati raj institutions and also the launching of externally aided projects in primary education, village education committees at various levels have been set up. Local, more specifically district primary educational plans are being formulated at decentralized levels. Their performance with respect to education development is well known. But there may not necessarily be a one to one relationship between decentralization.

Encouragement to Private Schools:

With respect to private schools, the present tendencies indicate that government favours in the name of 'building partnerships', the growth of private schools – both schools that are financially supported by the State as well as self – financing private schools. But the number of government aided school is decreasing. With the growth of such schools, the government might not feel the need for opening new government schools and as a result, the access of the poor to schools would be seriously affected. The Private schools promote dualism in education – an expensive system for the rich and a poor quality one for the poor. There is a strong need for the governments to substantially increase their spending on education with a strong political will.

Beti Bachao Beti Padhao Yojana

The Census (2011) data showed a significant declining trend in the Child Sex Ratio (CSR), calculated as number of girls for every 1000 boys between age group of 0-6 years, with an all time low of 918 in 2011 from 976 in 1961. This is an alarming indicator for women disempowerment. It reflects both prebirth discrimination manifested through gender biased sex selection, and post birth discrimination against girls. Alarm by the sharp decline of girl child,

Beti Bachao Beti Padhao Yojana (save daughter, educate daughter) has been launched which is a scheme of Government of India, introduced by the Honorable Prime Minister in January 2015 for saving and empowering the girl child. In the scheme it has been announced that the village which has balanced sex ratio, will be awarded Rs. 1 crore. The scheme has focused on 100 Districts of the country which have low Child Sex Ratio to ensure survival, protection and education of the girl child.

In spite of the forceful intervention by a bastion of female privilege, feminist critics, constitutional guarantees, protecting laws and sincere efforts by the state governments and central government through various schemes and programmes over the last 66 years and above all, the United Nation's enormous pressure with regard to the uplift of the plight of women in terms education is still in the state of an enigma in India.

The 2011 census report indicates that literacy among women as only 54 percent it is virtually disheartening to observe that the literacy rate of women India is even much lower to national average, i.e. 65.38. The growth of women's education in rural areas and urban slums (including Jelepara) is very slow. This obviously means that still large women folk of our country are illiterate, the weak, backward and exploited. Moreover, education is also not available to all equally. Gender inequality is reinforced in education which is proved by the fact that the literacy rate for the women is only 54% against 76% of men as per 2011 Census.

Kanyashree Prakalpa : An initiative of Govt. of West Bengal

Though child marriages are prohibited in all over India under the Prohibition of Child marriage Act, 2006 (PCMA) but still the practice of the same is a continuous process. Kanyashree Prakalpa has been introduced by the honourable Chief Minister to promote the education of girls and to control over child marriages. This scheme seeks to improve the status of marginalized sections of the society by ensuring girls' stay in school and delay their marriages till at least age 18. It is based on Conditional Cash

Transfers. This scheme has two cash transfer components:

- The first is an annual incentive of Rs. 750 to be paid only on the condition that girls should be unmarried and bonafide student of a school.
- The second is a onetime grant of Rs. 25000 on the condition of being unmarried and registered in academic institutions.

National Education Policy 2020

The girl child has to tackle is the inherent bias favouring the male child in Indian households, which makes families unwilling to spend on the education of the girl child. The girl child is usually expected to learn domestic chores and help with housekeeping and caring for younger siblings. There is a perceptible difference in school dropout rates based on gender. Roughly one in every five girls enrolled drop out after class 8. The figures are connected to the onset of menstrual age in girls, where not just the availability but the actual functioning of safe and hygienic toilets becomes crucial for their continued education. As a girl child grows older, safety issues become even more pertinent, and a long journey to school often poses a real threat to life and liberty for the child, making continued education a hazardous proposition. In India, child marriage, too, remains an unfortunate reality; according to a UNICEF nearly 27% of girls get married under the age of 18 every year, and this is likely to be pushed up by 20% due to the COVID-19 induced lockdown and subsequent migrant crisis this year. All these myriad problems riddle a girl's life, stealing from her childhood, the fun-filled, care-free days of school that is every child's birthright. The New Education Policy (NEP) 2020, India's first education of the 21st century, could be a thin ray of hope for the seemingly unremitting darkness in the quest for girls' education. The policy seeks to address the many shortcomings of our existing education system and sets itself lofty ideals to this end. It endorses the UN Sustainable Development Goal 4, of free universal access to quality education, and promises to transform the Indian education system such that, by 2040, it will be second to none in the world.

Conclusion

Gender equality in society implies a society in which women and men enjoy the same opportunities, outcomes, rights and obligations in all spheres of life. Despite many developmental efforts, women are still much more likely to be poor and illiterate than men. They usually have less access to medical care, property ownership, credit, and training and in employment. They are far less likely to be politically active and far more likely to be victims of domestic violence compared to men. The discourse of development is incomplete without the overall development of women in all fields including healthcare, economic independence and education. There are several measures for addressing the problems of marginalized sections of the society especially for women at international, national and local levels but still there are lacunae in the policies and their implementation for the women.

For institutionalizing the issues, it is essential that both men and women are aware of their rights and responsibilities. Only the government orders cannot bridge this lack of awareness, leaving open the possibility that the gender roles can become a controversial issue, which affects the sustenance of the total programme. A comprehensive campaign is therefore, required to overcome this lack of awareness. Here, Non – Government Organisations can play an important role by organising workshops and seminars to make people, especially women, aware of their potentialities and catalyse them in taking greater role jointly in development work so that development can be of the people, for the people and by the people.

References

Dreze, J., and A.K. Sen, 1995, 'Basic Education as a Political Issue', *Journal of Educational Planning and Administration,* vol. 9, no. 1, January, 1-26.

Government of India, 2015, '*Beti Bachao Beti Padhao*', Ministry of Women and Child Development.

Haq, Zia, Dec 15, 2015,00.09 IST, 'India at 130 among 188 countries in human development, up 5 slots', *Hindustan Times*, New Delhi.

Kabeer, 1999, 'Resources, Agency, Achievements: Reflections on the Measurement of Women's Empowerment' in *Development and Change,* Vol. 30, 437.

Khongsdier, R.,2005, 'Maternal Education in Relation to the Indicators of Health and Development in Northeast India', in V. Narayana Reddy, S. Vijaya Kumar, and B. Nalini eds *Women in Development Challenges and Achievements,* Serials Publications, New Delhi.

Kiran Das Naik, E. and M. Aravinda Kumar, 2014, 'Education and Women Empowerment in India' in Nagaraju Battu et al eds *Empowerment of Women in India New Strategies,* Regal Publications, New Delhi.

Nalini, B. And S. Elango, 2005, in Narayana Reddy, V. et.al eds *Women in Development Challenges and Achievements*, Serial Publications, New Delhi,231.

Nanda A.R. and Almas Ali (2006), 'Health Sector Issues and Challenges', in *India Social Development Report*, Council for Social Development, Oxford University Press, New Delhi, 26.

National Commission for Women (1996), *Annual Report, 1992 – 93 to 1996*, National Commission for Women, New Delhi.

Tyagi and Chatterjee,2005, 'Women in Development', in Narayana Reddy, V. et.al eds *Women in Development Challenges and Achievements*, Serial Publications, New Delhi,42-43.

Retrieved from https://www.youthkiawaaz.com/2020/07/early-marriage-hampers-girls-education-in-india/accessed on 18.07.22.

CHAPTER THREE

Various Policies in Women Education from Traditional to Modernity

Mr. Uday Modak: Assistant Professor, Bhavan's Tripura College of Teacher Education (BTCTE) Bimangarh, Narasingarh, Agartala, Tripura

Introduction

What does it mean to be a woman? First of all, a woman is a mother, a wife, a daughter, a friend. The woman is sensitive but also strong. The woman exudes beauty, sensuality, love. There is a woman standing behind any successful man and she experiences every feeling along him.

Women are true heroes who fight for their purposes, who go through life with their heads up and who love to be respected and appreciated. They are good friends and have compassion for each other. They are mothers who fight for their children, who sacrifice themselves for them. Women are the smile, the finesse and the love in this world. They have enormous soul power. Most of the time, women prefer to ignore ranking themselves as personalities, because they are always taking care of the people around her. Without some education and encouragement, they devalue themselves, we decided to come to their aid and give them an educational base to help them fulfill their dreams and goals.

Education is one of the most critical areas of empowerment for women, as both the Cairo and Beijing conferences affirmed. It is also an area that offers some of the clearest examples of discrimination women suffer. Among children not attending school there are twice as many girls as boys, and among illiterate adults there are twice as many women as men. Offering girls basic education is one sure way of giving them much greater power

-- of enabling them to make genuine choices over the kinds of lives they wish to lead. This is not a luxury. That women might have the chance of a healthier and happier life should be reason enough for promoting girls' education. However, there are also important benefits for society as a whole. An educated woman has the skills, information and self-confidence that she needs to be a better parent, worker and citizen.

An educated woman is, for example, likely to marry at a later age and have fewer children. Cross-country studies show that an extra year of schooling for girls reduces fertility rates by 5 to 10 per cent. And the children of an educated mother are more likely to survive. In India, for example, the infant mortality rate of babies whose mothers have received primary education is half that of children whose mothers are illiterate. An educated woman will also be more productive at work -- and better paid. Indeed, the dividend for educational investment is often higher for women than men. Studies from a number of countries suggest that an extra year of schooling will increase a woman's future earnings by about 15 per cent, compared with 11 per cent for a man.

2.0 Objectives of the study:

1. The study wills emphasis the various importance of Women Education.

2. To highlight various ways to create such an awareness towards various policies and periods of Women Education.

3. The study will suggest the uses, nature and scope of Women Education.

4. The study will discuss about the various benefits and drawbacks associated with Women Education.

5. The study will conduct how we can promote Women Education.

6. The study will describe various uses of Women Education.

3.0 Use of Education:

Women have a very in-distinctive position in our economy and are an indispensable part of the society. Yes, education and knowledge empower women. The only way a society or nation can move forward, and aspire to economic growth and development is not just through education- but especially education among the women citizens.

"To awaken the people, it is the women who must be awakened. Once she is on the move, the family moves, the village moves, the nation moves." - Pt. Jawaharlal Nehru

Education is a milestone of women empowerment because it enables them to respond to challenges, to confront their traditional role and change their life. Education is one of the ways to spread the message of women empowerment. Education not only educates a person but also helps her realize that she is a vital part to the society. Occupational achievement, self-awareness and satisfaction are among the many things that will be ensured by effective use of education. Guidance and counseling also provided through education, helps women select their jobs and build career paths. Education will help women to empower through the knowledge of science and technology to face the challenges of today's technological age. It also helps them in garnering information through the computer all over the world. Education not only educates a woman but enables her to take decisions and accept responsibilities at her home and outer world. Education helps a woman to understand her rights to equal treatment like a man in the society of this nation.

4.0 Women Education in Vedic Period:

Most females were allowed to pursue education without significant constraints in the Vedic period. Women's education, unlike in the subsequent periods was not neglected. Female scholars were also present during this period. The educators of this period had divided women into two groups - Brahmavadinis and Sadyodvahas. The former were life-long students of philosophy and theology. Sadyodvahas used to continue their studies until they got married. There were many women poets and philosophers, such as Apala, Ghosha and Visvavara.

5.0 Women Education in British Period:

The Church Missionary Society tasted greater success in South India. The first boarding school for girls came up in Tirunelveli in 1821. By 1840 the Scottish Church Society constructed six schools with roll strength of 200 Hindu girls. When it was mid-century, the missionaries in Madras had included under its banner, 8,000 girls. Women's employment and education was acknowledged in 1854 by the East Indian Company's Programme: Wood's Dispatch. Slowly, after that, there was progress in female education, but it initially tended to be focused on the primary school level and was related to the richer sections of society. The overall literacy rate for women increased from 0.2% in 1882 to 6% in 1947.

In western India, Jyotiba Phule and his wife Savitribai Phule became pioneers of female education when they started a school for girls in 1848 in Pune. In eastern India, apart from important contributions by eminent

Indian social reformers like Raja Ram Mohan Roy, Ishwar Chandra Vidyasagar, John Elliot Drinkwater Bethune was also a pioneer in promoting women's education in 19th-century India. With participation of like-minded social reformers like Ramgopal Ghosh, Raja Dakshinaranjan Mukherjee and Pandit Madan Mohan Tarkalankar, he established Calcutta's (now Kolkata) first school for girls in 1849 called the secular Native Female School, which later came to be known as Bethune School. In 1879, Bethune College, affiliated to the University of Calcutta, was established which is the oldest women's college in Asia.

In 1878, the University of Calcutta became one of the first universities to admit female graduates to its degree programmes, before any of the British universities had later done the same. This point was raised during the Ilbert Bill controversy in 1883, when it was being considered whether Indian judges should be given the right to judge British offenders. The role of women featured prominently in the controversy, where English women who opposed the bill argued that Bengali women, whom they stereotyped as "ignorant" and neglected by their men and that Indian men should therefore not be given the right to judge cases involving English women. Bengali women who supported the bill responded by claiming that they were more educated than the English women opposed to the bill and pointed out that more Indian women had degrees than British women did at the time.

6.0 Independence India:

After India attained independence in 1947, the University Education Commission was created to recommend suggestions to improve the quality of education. However, their report spoke against female education, referring to it as: "Women's present education is entirely irrelevant to the life they have to lead. It is not only a waste but often a definite disability." However, the fact that the female literacy rate was at 8.9% post-Independence could not be ignored. Thus, in 1958, a national committee on women's education was appointed by the government, and most of its recommendations were accepted. The cruxes of its recommendations were to bring female education on the same footing as offered for boys.

Soon afterwards, committees were created that talked about equality between men and women in the field of education. For example, one committee on differentiation of curriculum for boys and girls (1959) recommended equality and a common curricula at various stages of their learning. Further efforts were made to expand the education system, and the Education Commission was set up in 1964, which largely talked about female education, which recommended a national policy to be developed by the government. This occurred in 1968, providing increased emphasis on female education.

7.0 Current Policies:

Before and after Independence, India has been taking active steps towards women's status and education. The 86th Constitutional Amendment Act, 2001, has been a path breaking step towards the growth of education, especially for females. According to this act, elementary education is a fundamental right for children between the ages of 6 and 14. The government has undertaken to provide this education free of cost and make it compulsory for those in that age group. This undertaking is more widely known as Sarva Shiksha Abhiyan (SSA).

Since then, the SSA has come up with many schemes for inclusive as well as exclusive growth of Indian education as a whole, including schemes to help foster the growth of female education. **The major schemes are the following:**

Mahila Samakhya Program: This program was launched in 1988 as a result of the New Education Policy (1968). It was created for the empowerment of women from rural areas especially socially and economically marginalized groups. When the SSA was formed, it initially set up a committee to look into this programme, how it was working and recommended new changes that could be made.

Kasturba Gandhi Balika Vidyalaya Scheme(KGBV): This scheme was launched in July, 2004, to provide education to girls at primary level. It is primarily for the underprivileged and rural areas where literacy level for females is very low. The schools that were set up have 100% reservation: 75% for backward class and 25% for BPL (below Poverty line) females.

National Programme for Education of Girls at Elementary Level (NPEGEL): This programme was launched in July, 2003. It was an incentive to reach out to the girls who the SSA was not able to reach through other schemes. The SSA called out to the "hardest to reach girls". This scheme has covered 24 states in India. Under the NPEGEL, "model schools" have been set up to provide better opportunities to girls.

Other educational routes

Newlyweds (women specifically) are educated on family planning, safe sex, and birth control in population control programs. In addition, the government has established rural health houses managed by local health workers. These health professionals travel to different areas in order to impart information about women's health and birth control.

Raising awareness

The Canadian start-up Decode Global has developed the mobile game Get Water!, a game for social change focusing on the water scarcity in India and the effect it has on girls' education, especially in slums and rural areas. In areas with no ready access to water, girls are often pulled out of school to collect water for their families.

8.0 Women Education in Modern Society:

After independence the scope for women increased and Women Education in Modern India widened. The period and after 1948 in India, highest priority was given to women education. Women Education in Modern India became the major concern for both the government and civil society as educated women can play a vital role in the development of the country. Thus there was a great upsurge in awareness regarding women's rights among all sections of society. Various developmental programmes and policies were introduced in order to improve the social status of women. Education is creditable as it is beneficial for women as this reduces female infant mortality and child mortality rates.

In India the educational system was modified and three-tier instruction process was developed. All citizens of India are offered the right to education and Women Education in Modern India was opened to a new vista. The structure of Indian education system came into being. Two important structures came into being: formal and Non-Formal Education programme. Various other educational programmes such as online education and distance education were also launched. The main aim of all the educational programmes is to make every girl child of the society literate.

At present, Women Education in Modern India has achieved a new height. Currently, entrance of women in engineering, medical and other professional colleges is overwhelmingly elevated. Most of the professional colleges in the country keep thirty percent of the seats reserved for females. In urban India, girls are opened to a far wider scope then the rural girls.

In cultural reality, the women enjoyed a privileged position in the Vedic period. The women had special customs, rituals and spirituality, with which men were not allowed to interfere. In medieval period though women had to suffer because of various foreign interferences, yet in modern times the condition of women developed gradually. Moreover, Women Education in Modern India increased the intellectuality of the Indian women. Indian history produces famous women saints, healers and priests. For instance Andal, a 6th century A.D. sage and Jnanananda Ma of the 20th century have contributed to the society.

9.0 Conclusion:

Today the modern woman is totally different from what she used to be. She tries to constantly improve her position in society, she is preoccupied with her looks, and what is very important, she is trying to have a normal life without being constrained by anyone or anything. She has the right to express her opinion without fearing that someone will punish her for that. The modern woman wants good education and a blooming professional life, a way of life that allows her to have a baby and she can do it alone if she does not find the right man to support her. Over the years, there have been several women who are now considered to have made revolutionary changes in the global development. Strong and characterful have become role models and ideals for all feminine generations of all time. Everyone has noticed something different either that they have something to say, to accomplish, to show they have managed to mark forever the evolution of women in society.

India is now a leading country in the field of women education. History of India is never blank of brave women however it is full of women philosophers like Gargi, Viswabara, Maritreyi (of Vedic age) and other famous women are like Mirabai, Durgabati, Ahalyabi, Laxmibai, etc. All the famous historical women in India are inspiration for the women of this age. We never forget their contributions to the society and country.

References:

1. Achievement since Independence : girls Education". Archived from the original on 2011-10-

15.

2. "Educational Status of Women in the Vedic Period: An Introduction" (PDF).

3. Gachukia, Edduh (1995). The Education of Girls and Women in Africa. Nairobi: Forum for

African Women Educationalists

4. Ghosh, Ratna (2015). "Women's Empowerment and Education: Panchayats and Women's

Self-Help Groups in India". Policy Futures in Education. 13 (3): 294–314.

5. Hollos, Marida (1998). "The Status of Women in Southern Nigeria: Is Education a Help or a

Hindrance?" Women and Education in Sub-Saharan Africa: 247–277.

6. J. K. Sowards, Erasmus and the Education of Women Sixteenth Century Journal, Vol. 13, No.

4 (Winter, 1982), pp. 77-89

7. Kabeer, Naila. "Gender Equality And Women's Empowerment: A Critical Analysis Of The Third Millennium Development Goal." Gender & Development 13, no. 1 (2005): 13-24.

8. Khoja-Moolji, Shenila (2015). "Suturing Together Girls and Education: An Investigation Into

the Social (Re)Production of Girls' Education as a Hegemonic Ideology". Diaspora, Indigenous, and Minority Education. 9 (2): 87–107.

9. Stromquist, Nelly P. (2015). "Women's Empowerment and Education: linking knowledge to

transformative action". European Journal of Education. 50 (3): 307–324

10. S. P. Agrawal; J. C. Aggarwal (1992). Women's Education in India: 1986-1987. Concept

Publishing Company. p. 31. ISBN9788170223184.

11. Sarikhani, Nahid (April 2013). "The Study of Effects of Education on Women's Occupation in India". International Journal of Educational Sciences. 5 (2): 151–157.

12. William Lavely, Xiao Zhenyu, Li Bohua and Ronald Freedman (1990). The Rise in

Female Education in China: National and Regional Patterns. The China Quarterly, 121, pp 61-93

CHAPTER FOUR

Role of Parents, Teachers and Society in Promoting Mental Health of Students

Dr. Priti Chandorkar: Associate Professor, Gandhi Shikshan Bhavan's, Smt. Surajba College of Education, Mumbai, Maharashtra, priti.chandorkar@gandhishikshan.com

Abstract

According to WHO (1948) also, "Health could be a state of complete physical, mental and social well- being and not just the absence of wellness or infirmity". Time and again, the two vital classes of health that are examined totally are mental and physical health. Each mental and physical health are equally vital, neither one will overshadow the significance of the other. An individual who has good physical health is probably going to operate normally in any respective level of life. However, mental health is the state of mind in which an individual realizes his own potentialities. He can battle with the normal stress of life and can contribute in a conducive manner not solely in life but can also make some fruitful contribution towards his community too. Factors like depression, stress and anxiety can all effect mental health and destroy a person's routine life. It is seen that a large number of students are suffering from mental depression today. It is necessary to have mental health like physical health. Therefore, special emphasis has been laid on mental health at present. It is especially important to keep the mental health of the new generation or students intact. Current students are suffering from stress due to education and various problems of daily life. As a result, students are suffering from mental illness. Therefore, teachers and all family members should be aware to protect the mental health of the child or student.

Keyword: Mental Health, mental health, mental state, family, psychological, temperament, emotion, well-adjusted. Environment, Child

Introduction

Nowadays we are all more or less aware of physical health. But many people are not aware of what is meant by mental health, how to maintain the health of human health. Although many educators have a positive attitude about the importance and necessity of some human health sciences, it has not been long since it appeared as a collected scripture. At the same time, just as every human being has his own self-world, so he has various elements or objects around him, in which by coordination and interaction he grows, moves forward, and the functioning of the whole body, the ability to regulate and manifested. Mental health is an aspect of a person's overall health. Mental health is a combination of a person's physical health and mental health. In daily life, family, social, economic, political, educational events have affected our mental health. It puts stress on the mind in many ways that can disrupt mental well-being. The science of mental health is the science that is constantly working and researching to keep a person's mental health normal. With the overall development of the individual, the organization is constantly working towards the goal of serving. Maintaining mental health is a very important program in the life of an individual. Home and school play an important role in maintaining the mental health of the individual. As a social being, we are born into a family and participate in school education to receive education after family life. The family environment and the school environment affect the mental health of the student. An independent, stress-free, empathetic family environment and school environment help protect the mental health of the student.

Concept of Mental Health

Mental health is a joyful activity of the person's personality organization. The mental health of the person develops through the proper adjustment with environment. There are several positive things associated with healthy and normal mentality, such adjustment with changing environments, preparing the field of self-guidance, helping the individual to be establishment as a cohesive and ideal etc. Mental health helps a person to develop a balanced mental organization and adapt to the changing environment. According to J.A. Hadfield, "Mental Health is the full and free expressions of all our native and acquired potentialities in harmony with one another by being directed towards a common end aim of the personality as a whole."

Nature of Mental Health

Self-realization: One of the characteristics of mental health is self-realization. This means that a person can effectively realize himself, be able to read, write and speak. A philosophical vision will awaken in the person. The person will listen attentively to different topics and will be able to observe them. Will try to understand and protect about physical and mental health. Be aware of the person's ability to get what they want. Such a person will be entitled to a healthy lifestyle.

Able to establish human relationships: Another important feature of mental health is the establishment of human relationships. A mentally healthy person enjoys a diverse social life, Works in harmony with each other and tries to maintain democratic relations with other. Thus, establishes human relations. The decision is made by the person himself and he tries to maintain it firmly. He can tolerate a certain amount of stress which can keep the frustration at bay.

Responsible personality: Having a responsible personality is one of the characteristics of a healthy mindset. In other words, the mindset of taking responsibility and the harmony of the people in the preparation of the appropriate field to fulfill it is absolutely necessary. Responsible personalities place more importance on being aware of the health of all, being gracious towards individual differences, being loyal to the law and so on.

Mental health is both body and mind: mental health is not limited to the mind. Mental health depends on both the body and the mind. Because there is a close relationship between body and mind. When the body is sick, the normality of the mind, spontaneity, balance is likely to be disturbed. In other words, in order to keep mental health intact, both body and mind must be kept healthy.

Mental health is a dynamic concept: Mental health identifies the balance of the mind. Various events in a person's life disturb a person's mental balance. That is why the process and change of the correlation of the individual becomes necessary. That is, since the environment is changeable and mental health is dependent on the environment, mental health is a dynamic concept.

Self-evaluation: Self-evaluation is an important feature of mental health. Mental health informs about a person's abilities. Mental health makes a person aware of himself from different angles. In addition to being aware of a person's abilities, the person makes an accurate assessment of the limitations. In other words, we can say that a person with mental health can do self-evaluation.

Intellectual and emotional maturity: Intellectual maturity is another important feature of mental health. Mental health can be observed in the whole person and distorted intellectual development is also appropriate. In results intellectual and emotional maturity regularly spread knowledge, awaken a sense of responsibility, and bring clarity to the expression of thoughts and feelings.

High Adjustment Ability: High adjustment Ability is one of the main features of mental health. Everyone has to adapt to the changing environment. Attempts to adapt to changing environments are seen in individuals with mental health. Mental health can be impaired if a person is unable to adapt properly to his or her environment.

Improved way of life: better life and philosophy have the qualities of healthy mental health. Living according to the realities of the world and one's own abilities and determining one's needs are the marks of an improved way of life.

Foundations of Mental Health

Sound mental health relies on certain foundations. General physical health, psychological atmosphere and the sociological atmosphere lay the foundations for sound mental health. It had been Coleman (1956) who pin pointed these basic foundations of mental health.

General health: The physically healthy individual is less prone to malady than one who is in poor physical condition. The former can withstand psychological stresses and strains more steadily than the latter. Good physical health therefore lays a strong foundation for good mental state. General health study can facilitate the early detection and treatment of specific physical conditions that may lead to mental disabilities. So brain tumors, syphilis and certain alternative organic conditions could also be treated on time so as to avoid serious mental illness. Studies have shown that a large variety of biological conditions such as faulty genes, diseases, endocrine glands imbalance, malnutrition etc. interfere with normal growth and become the causes for maladjusted behaviour. Three genetic defects of major concern are bodily aberrations, faulty genes and genetic predisposition to specific mental disorders. Most of the knowledge concerning the role of genes in mental disorders relies on the study of family trees. Kallman (1958) studied the inheritance of schizophrenia.

Findings show that the incidence of schizophrenia is much higher among blood relations than within the general population.

Deformities and imperfections of body such as gimp, deafness, vision defect and crookedness, etc. whether inborn or accidental can be factors effecting mental health. However, the importance of a physical impairment depends totally on the approach the individual evaluates and adjusts thereto. Common undesirable reactions to physical handicaps are feelings of inferiority, sorrow and hostility. As a consequence, the individual might develop psychological handicaps that are much more disabling than his physical impairment.

Physical deprivation such as deficiency disease, sleep etc. are important factors concerning mental health. The actual fact that deficiency disease in early life effects intellectual development has been reported by the International Commission on Education in their report entitled 'Learning to Be'. In line with Adelson, two out of every three hospitalized mental patients have suffered severe sleep disturbances before being hospitalized. Also, emotional processes like worry and anger mobilize body resources to satisfy emergency situations, prolonged mobilization of such kind produces physiological changes that ultimately harm the organism. Further, it is calculated that 50% of patients suffer from brain pathology. This could be temporary as in the case of drug intoxication or it should be permanent as just in case of syphilitic infection of brain.

Psychological conditions: Infants bereft of maternal love and care later develop mental health issues. Such deprivation could result because of separation from mother and placement of the kid in any establishment, placement in foster homes etc. Such kids are deprived of encouragement and positive learning. A study conducted by Beres and Overs in1950 on thirty-seven adolescents institutionalized for thirteen years. At the time of study sixteen or eighteen years after discharged from the orphanage, four were diagnosed as psychotic, twenty-one had character disorder, four were mentally retarded, two were neurotic and seven were normal. Severe and sustained maternal deprivation of kids inside the home too can seriously retard overall development of the individual.

Infancy and early childhood are crucial stages of an individual's development during which he requires the gratification of many desires to assure good adjustment. During later childhood too, the kid must not experience rejection through physical neglect, denial of love and affection, lack of interest in the kid's activities and achievements, harsh, inconsistent punishment and failure to spend time with the kid. Another psychological facet which lays the base for sound mental state is the extent of protection the kid gets from the family. Overshielding from the slightest risk could hamper the kid's growth. Jenkins reported in a study that kids referred to clinics had insecure mothers. On the other hand, over indulged, over permissive parents can lead to children becoming spoiled, selfish, inconsiderate and stern. Seers reported that high permissiveness and low punishment within the home were related absolutely with delinquent aggressive behaviour.

Over and on the top of most psychological factors, the type of family structure lays the essential foundation of mental state. Psychologists have pin pointed four patterns of family structure which can be harmful to the mental state of an individual-

- The inadequate family is characterized by the lack of ability to address the standard issues of family living. It lacks physical and psychological resources for meeting its problems and depends heavily upon continued outside assistance. Thus, it cannot give feeling of safety and security to kids.
- The disturbed family has parents who are grossly eccentric and in an exceeding state of constant emotional turmoil. Parents fight to take care of their own equilibrium and the kid does not get the required love and guidance. Almost inevitably, the kid gets intermeshed in the emotional conflicts of parents.
- The delinquent family inculcates values not accepted by the broader community. Kids in these families are inspired in dishonesty, deceit and alternative undesirable behaviour.
- The discontinuous families are incomplete whether or not as a result of death, divorce, separation or some other conditions. All these families are predisposing to mental health.
- Besides the above, a couple of alternative psychological aspects related to mental state are a sense of failure, losses, guilt, loneliness, value conflict, conformity versus nonconformity and avoiding versus facing reality. There are several losses that individual invariably experience- losses involving objects or individuals with whom they powerfully establish, loss of money, social prestige etc. tend to devalue an individual in his own eyes as well as in the eyes of others.

Sociological foundations: It is rather tough to draw a transparent line of demarcation between the psychological and sociological aspects of mental health. Almost invariably psychological issues are precipitated out from the sociological context and conditions. In modern times significantly, there is cut-throat competition in society in all walks of life such as academics, sports, job and even in getting marital partners. The constant struggle to induce success creates tension and anxiety. In the field of education, long hours of study, examination tension and sustained concentration of effort over a few years leads to considerable stress for several students. Jobs, on the line of work create severe demand in terms of responsibility, time and performance. Wedding and family conjointly make serious demands from the partners concerned. War and violence, riot etc. in society place a lot of people under stress since these destabilize and disorganize society. Also, group prejudice that manifests itself in the protraction of communal feelings and discrimination on the ground of caste, creed and region tends to debase and confuse people. Children retarded in such settings have a significant task attempting to learn what is predictable and possible, of striving to develop healthy motives and values and of making an attempt to attain academic and other competencies essential for effective participation in society. Inflation, unemployment and job discontentment are sources of mental stress for many individuals in society. Depression, suicide and crime increase because of the unemployment. Job discontentment creates stress and anxiety and a wide range of psychological disorders.

In 1962, Srole et.al have shown that mental disease is higher among individuals from lower socio-economic status than from those in the higher levels of the socio-economic ladder. In addition, Rosen and Gregory (1965) have shown that single or unmarried person tends to be more prone to mental illness compared to the ones who are happily married. However, a lot of analysis must be carried out to spot the exact influence of sociological factors on mental disease. Intensive studies on the social backgrounds of mentally disturbed persons, cross-cultural studies on mental illness and how numerous socio -cultural factors contribute to the development of serious mental disorders need to be executed. In the future, with such a body of information, we could be able to develop sociological preventive measures that combat mental illness, just as we have been able to subdue epidemics of physical malady by applying public health measures.

Role of Parents, Teachers and Society in promoting Mental Health

No two individuals are alike. Even identical twins differ to a great extent in physical, emotional, intellectual, social, moral aspects of development. These variations are due to the interactional process of nature and nurture. These variations influence the adaptability of the individuals to their surrounding and effect their mental state. So, the role of parents, faculty and society in promoting mental health is appreciable.

ax. Early interaction of the child with parents features a nice influence on his mental development. A baby begins life in a state of virtually complete helplessness and is totally reliant on his parents or significant others to gratify his desires which are physiological in nature. Parents ought to instill fascinating traits in kids and develop competence, security, adequacy, vanity and discipline.

ax. School features a crucial role in balanced temperament development. Providing varied opportunities for overall development of the potentialities of scholars will cause their fulfillment and prevent mental disorders. Further, identification of emotionally disturbed students and providing remedial programmes for them is additionally a responsibility of schools.

ax. Society features a responsibility to produce situations for emotional expression of individuals. An individual right from his birth to death remains in close association with society. For harmonious development of temperament, social interaction is vital. In the process of social adjustment, the normal expression of feelings is crucial for mental health. There ought to be no repression of feelings as it ends up in abnormality. Society ought of offer socially acceptable channels for release of repressed emotional feelings in order that proper adjustment takes place.

ax. Positive approach towards work develops mental health. Work ought to be administered with pleasure and not as if it were a burden. It is the responsibility of parents and academicians to envision that young child develop a positive approach to do whatever has been assigned to them.

Conclusion

In order for a person to live a healthy life, human health needs to remain intact. You have to be physically fit as well as mentally healthy. Parents and academicians ought to facilitate the child to grasp himself-realize about his body and mind. The child must conjointly recognize the realities of life. However, mere knowing oneself is not enough. It should be supplemented by accepting oneself and being oneself. It is the duty of not just academician, but also parents to develop an objective attitude in children to understand themselves. Children should be helped to line life goals in accordance with their potentialities to avoid frustration. Well, human health has to improve and we have to move towards proper development. Improving mental health will lead to better personality development and betterment of society and country.

References

- Ghosh, S. K. (2014). Sikshay Sangati- Apasangati O Nirdesana.Kolkata: Classic books
- Nag, S. & Dutta, G. (2012). Guidance and Counselling in Adjustment. Kolkata: Rita Book Agency
- Pal, D. (2007). Guidance And Counselling. Kolkata: Central Library
- Chatterjee, B. M. & Mukherjee, R. (2017). Kolkata: Aaheli Publishers
- Mondal, V.(2012). Nirdeshana O Paramarshodaner Ruprekha. Kolkata: Rita Publication
- State Government of Victoria. Promoting mental health and wellbeing in your school. Retrieved on 3rd July,2021 from https://www.education.vic.gov.au/school/teachers/health/mentalhealth/Pages/promoting-mental-health.aspx
- Swapnajaidupally & Kiran, V. K. (2018). Role of school in child's mental health. International Journal of Multidisciplinary Research and Development, e-ISSN: 2349-4182 from https://www.researchgate.net/publication/324965264_Role_of_school_in_child's_mental_health
- Mental Health America. What Every Child Needs For Good Mental Health. Retrieved on 3rd July,2021 from https://mhanational.org/what-every-child-needs-good-mental-health
- Playgroup NSW. Effective Ways of Promoting Mental Health In Young Children. on 3rd July,2021 from https://www.playgroupnsw.org.au/ParentResources/Health/promoting-children%E2%80%99s-mental-health

A Comparative Study on Perceptions of Women on Gender Discrimination, Biases, and Stereotype in the 21st Century.

Sarthak Paul, Research Scholar, Mahatma Gandhi University, 13th Mile, G.S. Road, Khanapara, Dist-Ri-Bhoi, Meghalaya, sarthak.paul650@gmail.com, 9775840616

Abstract

As a country with a very long and rich civilization, India worships women as goddesses. However, there are discrimination, bias, and stereotypes against women in our society from a very early age. While we tell ourselves that our society is modern, we still see female infanticide, dowry, and early girl marriage. Gender discrimination is a curse in society. However, we still see these in society. These malpractices can easily hinder the growth of a country in society. In the 21st century, we still divide work according to gender. This study tried to determine what kinds of gender discrimination were found based on women's perceptions. It will be a comparative study that will help us know why gender discrimination still exists in society and the possible solutions to these problems.

Keywords: Gender, Gender discrimination, Gender stereotype, gender bias, women empowerment.

Introduction:

India is a very old civilized country. India is a country where we worship women as goddesses. However, we see gender discrimination, gender bias, and stereotypes in society very early. We tell ourselves modern, but we still see female infanticide, the dowry system, early girl marriage, etc., in our society.

We call our society male dominant society. We often see gender discrimination, gender bias, and stereotypes in our society. Nevertheless, what women think about gender discrimination, gender bias, and stereotypes is the primary topic for discussion in this study. In this study, the investigator tried to find women's perceptions of gender discrimination, biases, and stereotype in the 21st century based on their responses.

Conceptual framework:

Gender: Gender can also be defined by social constructs such as gender roles and norms. These are the roles, behaviours, and values that a society considers appropriate for men and women.

Gender discrimination: Generally, gender discrimination refers to the unequal or disadvantageous treatment of an individual or group of individuals since it relates to gender. It may involve academic programs, discipline, and class assignments in the classroom that treat an individual differently based upon their gender.

Gender stereotype: Associating specific characteristics, behaviours, or roles to a woman or a man based solely on the fact that he or she belongs to a particular social group implies gender stereotypes.

Gender bias: In general, gender bias refers to favouring one gender over another, for example, preferring men or boys to women or girls. It is a tendency to prefer one gender over the other.

Women empowerment: The term female empowerment can refer to many things, including accepting women's viewpoints or looking for them and increasing the status of women through education, awareness, literacy, and training.

Objectives:

- To study the perception of women regarding the perfect age for marriage based on their types of children, age and educational qualification.
- To Study how women perceive who can look after their parents better before and after marriage based on their type of children, age, and education.

- To study the perception of women regarding the fascination of a male or a female child based on their type of children, age, and education.
- To study the perception of women regarding studies and jobs of their children based on their type of children, age, and education.

Common gender discrimination, gender bias and gender stereotype in school and society:

- Often, male teachers spend more time interacting with boys.
- Often, teachers are harsher on boys than girls when they commit similar mistakes.
- In a school program, girls are often encouraged to sing; dance and, boys are encouraged to participate in aggressive sports and girls in soft sports.
- In a school function, boys are encouraged to do hard work and girls to do soft work.
- Often, teachers encourage boys to choose science and girls to choose arts.
- Female teachers get priority to teach in primary school.
- Females are seen as the ones who take care of the house from the inside, and boys are the ones who take care of the house from the outside.
- Females are expected to be soft-hearted and males are rough and tough.
- Females are expected to wear Shari, Churidar, and Bangles; males to wear shirts and pants.

Methodology:
In a nutshell, the research method is the science of researching how research is conducted. Above all, it refers to a systematic method of exploring the research problem. To conduct the research efficiently, the researcher must be familiar with both the research method and the research methodology, determining the steps they take.

Method: The research method used in this study was a descriptive study.

Sampling: Stratified random sampling and judgemental sampling were used For collecting the data.

Sampling size:
Women having children or no children Sample Size
Women having only male child/children 8
Women having only female child/children 8
Women having both male and female children 16

Women having no children or unmarried 9
Sample distribution based on types of children
Age of the women Sample Size
<35 18
35-55 16
>55 7
Sample distribution based on age
Educational Qualification Sample Size
School-level education 22
Graduation-level education 14
Master or Higher-level education 5
Sample distribution based on educational qualification
Data collection tools: A non-standardized researcher-made tool used for data collection. Data was collected through the interview schedule method.
Data analysis and Interpretation:

A. **Based on types of children:**

- It is seen that 37.5% of women having only male children are fascinated with having a male or a female child before marriage. However, the fascination has increased to 62.5% after their marriage. It is seen that 50% of women having only female children are fascinated with having a male or a female child before marriage. However, the fascination has decreased to 25% after their marriage. The study found that 18.75% of women who had both male and female children had a fascination with male and female children before they married, but this fascination dropped to 0% after they married; 33.33% of women without children had a fascination with giving birth to a female child in the future.
- Women's ages tended to be lower than boys' ages in every response we got from them regarding marriage age. Women's average marriage age should be 24, 24.5, 23, and 25 based on the responses the investigator got from the women having only male children, only female children, male and female children, and no children, respectively. Moreover, men's average marriage age should be 29, 29, 27.5, and 28.5, based on the responses the investigator got from the women having only male children, only female children, male and female children, and no children.

- When asked what kind of characteristics they want to see in future children? There was no discrimination; they all agreed that children should be good humans. A few added, however, that women should have a soft heart.

- 50%, 62.5%, 68.75%, and 55.55% of women agreed that daughters looked after their parents better before their marriage based on the responses the investigator got from the women having only male children, only female children, both male and female children, and no children respectively. 0%, 25%, 12.5%, and 22.22% of women believed that sons looked after their parents better based on the responses, respectively. 25%, 12%, 18.75%, and 0% agreed that both sons and daughters could look after their parents well before marriage based on the responses, respectively. The rest of the women agreed that the sons want to look after their parents but cannot do so due to the immense pressures of work.

- Everyone having only male children agreed to send their children far away from home if they got an excellent opportunity for higher education or jobs. 50% of women with only female children wanted to send their daughters far away from home for studies if they had an excellent opportunity. However, the number increased to 75% when the women were asked if they allowed their daughters to get a job far away from home. 68.75% of women agreed to allow their daughters to go far away from home for studies and jobs, but 81,25% agreed to allow their sons to go far away from home for studies and jobs. Interestingly 12.5% agreed to allow their sons but not their daughters.

A. **Based on age:**

- Women were asked to respond about the perfect age for marriage. Women's average marriage age should be 24, 24.5, and 21 based on the responses the investigator got from the women aged less than 35, aged between 35-55, and aged greater than 55, respectively. And men's average marriage age should be 29, 28.5, and 26.5 based on the responses, respectively.

- Women were asked about a son or daughter who looked after their parents better before marriage. 77.78% of women whose age is less than 35 think daughters, and 14.28% think sons look after their parents better before the marriage. 62.5% of women aged between 35 to 55 think daughters, 18.75% think sons, and 18.75% think both look after their parents better before the marriage. 14.28% of women whose age is greater than 55 think daughters, 42.86% think sons, and 42.86% think both look after their parents before marriage

- A similar question was asked about a son or a daughter who looks after their parents better after marriage. 50% of women whose age is less than 35 think daughters, 22.22% think sons, and 27.78 think it depends on whether the daughters are employed, whether the house where they live after marriage is not very far away from their parents' house, whether the sons have well adjustable life partners. 25% of women between the ages of 35 to 55 think daughters, 18.75% think sons, and 50% think it depends on the issues discussed above. 100% of the women whose age is greater than 55 is believed that sons look after their parents better after the marriage of both sons and daughter.

- 83.33% and 88.89% of women whose age is less than 35 are happy to allow their children to go far away from home for studies and jobs, respectively. 68.75% and 75% of women aged between 35 to 55 are happy to allow their children to go far away from home for studies and jobs, respectively. 71% and 71% of women whose age is greater than 55 are happy to allow their daughters to go far away from home for studies and jobs. But the numbers increased to 100% when the same question was asked about their sons.

C. **Based on educational qualification:**

- According to women with only school-level education, the ideal age for girls to get married is 23; for boys, it is 28. Women with graduation-level education thought it was 25 and 29 for girls and boys, respectively. The women with master-level education thought it was 24 and 30 for girls and boys, respectively.

- 68.18% of women having only school-level education thought that daughters could look after their parents better before the marriage; 13.64% thought sons and 18.18% thought both could look after their parents well before the wedding. 64.29% of women with graduation level education thought daughters could look after their parents better; 14.29% thought sons and 14.29% thought both could look after their parents well before marriage. 60% of women with master-level education thought that daughters could look after their parents better.

20% thought males and 20% thought it depends on circumstances when asked who can look after their parents better before the marriage.

- 27.27% of women having only school-level education thought that daughters could look after their parents better after marriage; 40.90% thought sons, 22.27% thought both sons and daughters could look after their parents better after marriage. 4.55% felt that it depended on circumstances. 50% of women having graduation-level education thought daughters could look after their parents better after marriage; 28.57 thought sons and 14.29% thought both could look after their parents well after the wedding. 7.14 % thought it depended. 20% of women having master-level education thought sons could look after their parents better. 40% thought both could look after reasonably, and 20% believed it depended on the circumstances.

- 63.64% of women having only school-level education agreed to allow their children to go far away from home for education or studies. 93.86% of women having graduation-level education decided on the same. The 80% of women having master-level education agreed on whether they would allow their children to go far away from home for studies or education.

Findings:

- The fascination with the girl-child is visible among women aged less than 35. Earlier, we saw the desire of the male child among women, but now the passion of the girl child has immersed among the young women rapidly.

- It is visible that women's ages tended to be lower than boys' ages in every response the investigator got from them regarding marriage age. It shows that gender bias, discrimination, and stereotypes still exist regarding marriage age. Women still believe that men's age has to be higher than women's age in marriage. But, one woman did not mention any age of male or female for marriage. She said that males or females should marry after standing on their own feet.

- Gender bias, discrimination, and stereotype are visible in the women's responses when asked who could look after their parents before and after marriage. A standard percentage of the women said that daughters could not look after their parents after marriage if daughters were housewives. A typical portion of women believed that women look after their parents better before the wedding because boys are busier outside and girls inside the house.

- Although most women agreed to allow their children to go far away from home for studies and jobs; however, a few women still were not ready to send their daughters to go far away from home while preparing to do so for their sons.

Role of Schools and society to avoid gender discrimination, gender bias and gender stereotype:

- **Providing equal opportunity** is a very important step to avoiding such issues. In family, school, college, and society we have to stop discriminating against males and females based on their gender.
- **Mandatory participation in a particular task** irrespective of gender can be very helpful. Sometimes, it is seen that
- **Using nonbiased language** is a helpful technique to avoid such issues. We use such biases in our day-to-day life; like- girls have less intelligence, men cannot cry, women should be soft-hearted, etc. We need to avoid such language.
- **Providing nonbiased books** can be helpful in fighting against these problems. Often, we see in books that male farmers are working in the field, while women are doing household work. These need to be stopped.
- **Parents-Teacher meetings** should be organised to discuss these issues so that they do not show such behaviours which promote gender biases.

Importance of women empowerment to Irradicate such issues:
Empowering women can be very helpful to solve many social problems, like:

- **Increasing Girl's education:** Often parents see their male children as the earner of the future. But an empowered woman can also run a family. In this study, many women believed that empowered women can look after their parents better.
- **Increasing female marriage age:** Very often we see women getting married at 18. Empowering women will make the parents realize that it is a very early time for marriage. It will help to minimise the fertility, and childbirth mortality rate.

- **Erasing dowry system:** Empowering women will help to erase the dowry system. The government is trying to abolish the dowry system for a long time, but it exists in society. Empowering women is the only way forward to stop the dowry system.
- **Establishing equality in society:** A society cannot run properly without empowering women. We shout for equality in society, but without empowering women it is not possible.

Conclusion:

A standard percentage of women believe that gender discrimination and gender biases still exist in this study because girls are not empowered. So, it is very much important to empower women. Only it is the way to eradicate these practices from society. With that, we need to spread awareness for girls' education. Some old laws regarding girls' marriage need to be changed. We need to encourage girls to participate in those activities where society thinks girls cannot succeed.

"To the women of this country, I would say exactly what I say to the men. Believe in India and in our Indian faith. Be strong and hopeful and unashamed."- Swami Vivekananda.

References:

Contributors to Wikimedia projects. (2015, September 17). *Women's empowerment-Wikipedia*. Wikipedia, the Free Encyclopedia;

Shivalik, P. (2020). *Pedagogy And Child Development* (pp. 246–251). Invincible Publishers.

CHAPTER SIX

Women as Decision-making Leader

Biswajit Das: Faculty of Education, Dasarathi Hazra Memorial College, Bhatar, Purba Bardhaman

Abstract

Empowerment means giving someone power or authority. Women need freedom to take proper decisions without any social restrictions. The objectives of the study are to understand decision decision-making process; to evaluate role of education in building the women as decision-making leader, to analyze the barriers in decision-making process, to study critical steps of decision-making process. The present study mainly based on secondary data. The information has to be collected from books, published data of World Bank Report and research paper and journals that provides an entire scenario about women as decision-making leader. In conclusion the role of women in today's world is changing significantly. Earlier women were dependent on father or husband, but now they have become capable enough to take proper decisions in various complicated situations that lead to healthy and successful life. So women should be encouraged to learn new things and do something apart from the household works. They should be given equal opportunities in all fields. They should be given freedom of choosing their career and making their decision in life.

Keywords: Decision-making, Leadership, Education

Introduction:

Women's empowerment is a combination of the two words 'women' and empowerment'. Empowerment means giving someone power or authority. By educating each and every girl child is the right way to raise their voice against any abuse. Women need freedom to take their decisions without any social restrictions. The things needed for decision making in education, literacy, and training to help them improve their position. Empowering a women helps to improve the country's growth. Women are considered the backbone of a family. She handling the children, parent, cooking are multi task works. They are very efficient doing multi tasking at a time. Women are powerful. If she shows their ideas, strength or views in public someone called as 'Feminist'. A woman is the beautiful creation of God is a fact because great personalities are born from the women's womb.

A mother is the first teacher of a child. If women have no education how can they teach properly a child? The empowerment of the women is the most essential factor that helps to growth of the country. The society includes 50% men and 50% women. Men were considered important members of a family in olden day. His decision is the final decision of a family. They were responsible for earning for living. Empowerment of women now can be categorized into five. They are social, education, political, economic and psychological. Women must be educated for a healthy and a happy life. They do not have to depend on family for anything. Educated women will be aware of her right and she knew how to fight against social and domestic violence, dowry system, child marriage, poverty, low wages etc. Savitribai Phule was the first female teacher in Indian. She opened a school for girls with her husband Jyotirao Phule. They started school in Bhidewada in Pune city in the year 1848. They faced harassment from others because of this. Provide better education for girls and give equal wages in all sectors like men. Avoid child marriage and dowry system from our society. This will help women to come front in all field.

Objective of the study:

The following objectives of the study are as below:

- To understand the meaning of the decision-making process.
- To find out the factors that affect in leadership of women.
- To evaluate the role of education in building the women as decision-making leader.
- To study the critical steps of the decision making process.
- To analysis the barriers in decision-making process.
- To identify the role of women in modern society as decision-making leader.

Meaning of decision making process:

Decision-making can be regarded as the mental processes in the selection of a course of action among several alternatives. Every decision-making process produces a final choice.

According to Koontz and O'Donnell "Decision making is the actual selection from among alternatives of a course of action".

Selection of one alternatives out of different alternatives

The process of decision is about something important especially in a group of people or in an organization.

Decision making is the actual selection from among alternatives of a course of action.

Characteristics of decision making process:

The following characteristics of decision-making process are as below:

- It is a process of selecting the best from the alternatives.
- It is an important job of a manager; therefore it is done in a rational manner.
- It is based on manager's knowledge, experience, judgment, and creativity and innovation skill.
- It involved the evaluation of various available alternatives.
- It aimed at achieving organizational goals. It implies that decision-maker attempt to achieve some results through decision-making.
- It is situation in nature.
- It involves commitment.

Steps of decision making process:

The following steps of decision-making process are as below:

1. Identification of problem
2. Identification of alternatives
3. Evaluation of alternatives
4. Choose best alternative.
5. Implement the decision.
6. Evaluation decision.

Women as decision-making leader:

Women are important for the development of the society as well as the family. Women need to be empowered only then the belief of women to do anything will increase. Just as men in the family can take right decisions to make a work successful so, can girls and women. We or our patriarchy in this patriarchal society is depriving women to keep the nobility alive or to preserve the tradition. Women have the same rights as men in this world. Not only is the help of men needed for the development of our country but also the contribution of women. In earlier days women were not given much importance but with the change of time this gender disparity has to be removed only then every country will progress.

Women should be given opportunities in decision making process. Only then will the inner potential in girls emerge. The women of the family should be given responsibility for various matters. Encouragement should be given to participate in various activities of the society. Only the full development of self power will take place in women. Women cannot be underestimated in anything. There are some superstitions and conservative attitudes which are hindering the empowerment of women. Women's empowerment will flourish only when girls are given complete freedom, courage and confidence boost. To develop decision making capacity among women, girls need to receive proper education. Apart from this, arrangement must be made in a suitable environment, but also various complex situation and environment have to be given responsibility. As a result, students, women, and girls will learn to understand the real truth of life. Whenever women can gain real life experience then they will be able to take right and women will be empowered to lead healthy lives of their own.

Women in leadership:

It's time for the world to recognize the benefits of women in leadership, and commit to placing even more women in positions of power. Women are powerful agents of change, and the far-reaching benefits of diversity and gender parity in leadership and decision-making are increasingly recognized in all spheres. Still, women continue to be vastly under-represented in decision-making in politics, business and communities. Women as leaders and decision-makers at all levels are critical to advancing gender justice and gender equality and to furthering economic, social and political progress for all.

- When women are meaningfully represented and engaged in leadership bodies such as legislative, courts, executive boards, community council like laws, riling and decision are more likely to be inclusive, representative and take diverse views into account.

- Women's leadership within households, including decision-making over land and household income, improve access to education and healthcare for their families.
- Countries with a great proportion of women as top decision-makers in legislatives have lower levels of income inequality.
- Peace agreements are 35% more likely to last at least 15 years if women leaders are engaged in its creation and execution.
- When women hold more executive leadership positions, their companies are more profitable: companies in the top quartile for gender diversity on executive teams are 21%more likely to outperform the national average.

Role of education in decision-making leader as women:

Education, in itself is a dynamic process and can be received from various institutions. Schools are one such institution that aims at providing age-appropriate, structured learning to young people amalgamated with other activates that can be develop an individual holistically and enhance the happiness quotient along with the knowledge and skills required to lead a successful life. Schools, today operate in complex environments. The school system demand leaders to be effective instructional leaders. In the 21st century, a principal is often regarded as a professional leader of learning and is a active facilitator of change. They are the ones who adapt to the changing needs of education in the society and bring in reforms in the education systems. Thus school leaders are increasingly believed to be a significant contributing factor responsible for determining students' learning environment and school outcomes.

Education contributes immensely to an individual's decision making process. Educated person can take various decisions in any situation. Decision making is not an easy task but it is a powerful task. When taking a decision on any matter, one has to think about the situation around it. Deciding an anything is not an easy matter. It is necessary to think about the matter in order to take a decision in her life, women have to be brave and confident. In this case, education makes women face different situations in life which makes the women very confident and has no problem in making decisions about anything. The following are some of the things that help woman to increase her decision-making power in life.

1. Confidence of women:

Education does not mean moral knowledge; education means the real education of life, the real truth that we realize from life. The real lesson or truth of life given a women a huge boost in self-confidence which helps the women to take decisions as a leader.

2. Information about various subjects:

Proper education helps to learn about various things in life. And there is no difficulty in deciding anything. Information about various aspects of life helps to increase decision-making among women.

3. Giving adequate freedom to women:

The most important requirement for making a decision is sufficient freedom. If women are not given enough freedom they will not be able to make decisions and will be unable to make decisions. Therefore, to develop decision-making power among women, they need to be given sufficient freedom.

4. Empowerment of women:

Women should be empowered so that they can take their own decisions, not only that, the girls should not depend on other people to make decisions. So it is quite clear that women empowerment increases her decision-making power in her life.

5. Development of women's inner strength:

Women have inherent powers that need to be developed. Only then will women be strong from within. Weakness will diminish in him and lion courage will awaken and women will be empowered and able to make decisions.

Hurdles faced by women during effective decision-making process:

Effective decision-making is an art which obviously cannot be earned overnight, hence needs to be nurtured in time. However even an effective leader cannot remain oblivious to certain hurdles which chronicle her decision-making capacity. An effective decision has positive effects on all the departments, and equal damage is caused by an ineffective decision. Hence she has to remain vigilant about the repercussions caused by his decisions. Sometime taking a decision can equal to cracking a hard nut. As a professional as well as an individual, we face many situations in our professional as well as personal lives, wherein it is quite tough to take a decision. A careful study of various hurdles faced will lead us to take effective and better decisions in future.

Following are typical barriers faced by a manger as women while developing strategies.

1. Level of decision -making not clear:

Sometime there is ambiguity in the level of power a manager holds, whether she holds the right to make modifications in the existing system. This often leads to confusion in the minds of manager, especially at a middle-level manager.

2. Lack of time:

Hasty decisions often lead to disastrous effect. However business is subject to emergencies and often as a decision making authority, we need to take a call in the limited time available. This can pose a most difficult hurdle for most leaders; however an effective leader has to go through theses testing times.

3. Lack of reliable data:

Lack of reliable data can be a major hindrance in making apt decisions. Ambiguous and incomplete data often makes it difficult for them to make an appropriate decision, which may not be the best suited for any organization.

4. Risk-taking ability:

Any decision attracts a fair deal of risk of resulting into negative outcomes. However it is necessary to take calculated risk for an effective decision. Also at the same time casual attitude and completely ignoring risks will not result in taking appropriate decisions.

5. Too many options:

A manager can be in a dilemma if there are too many options for an effective solution. Finding the appropriate one can be very difficult, especially if a particular decision favors a department over the other.

6. Inadequate support:

A manager however good she may be cannot work without an adequate support level from his subordinates. Lack of adequate support either from top level or grass root level employees may result in a great jeopardy for the manger.

7. Lack of resources:

A woman may find it difficult to implement her decisions due to lack of resources, time, staff, and equipment. In these cases, she should look out for alternative approaches which fit in the available resources. However, appropriate steps must be taken in case she feel that lack of resources many stop the growth of the organization.

8. Inability to change:

Every organization has its own unique culture which describes itsworking policies. However, some policies are not conducive to managers who are looking out for a change. The rigid mentality of top-level management and the subordinates are the biggest hurdle, wherein a leader cannot make positive amendment even if she wishes to do so.

Every experience is a big teacher, and women should take a cure from their previous experience, and learn to boost their decision-making capacity. Big businesses have benefited greatly from positive changes and results, which implies that a woman should first and foremost improve his ability to deal with risks to take a good decision.

Benefits in modern society as decision-making leader:

Women are often dynamic leaders of change, galvanizing women and men to get involved, claim their rights, strengthen their communities and protect their planet. Their participation is fundamental to democratic governance. Yet women still have far to go towards equal representation in positions of power and leadership, whether in corporate boardrooms or presidential cabinets. Discriminatory laws and practices hold women back as do limits on education, income and time away from care giving. Just over 21 percent of parliamentarians are women up from around 11 percent when the Beijing Fourth World Conference on women took place in 1995. While women have made inroads in many areas, at the current place of change, we would not see gender parity in governments, parliaments of peace tables until the next century. The Beijing conference agreement, known as the platform for Action, dubbed women in power and decision making one of 12 critical areas of concern. It made two essential commitments to change. First it called for measures ensuring women's equal access to and full participation in power structures and decision-making. Political quotas or positive measures are example of these. By reserving seats of candidates for women, they have driven dramatic increase in the number of women leaders in some countries. Second, the Platform urged steps to increase women's ability to participate. Training on leadership, public speaking and political campaigning, for instance, grooms women to complete, win and be good leaders who can inspire others.

Women have a right to equal participation. Once in leadership roles, they can make a difference that benefits whole societies. The Inter-parliamentary Union has found that women politicians give more attention to social welfare and legal protections, and improve trust. Taking up the Beijing commitments and rallying around women's leadership could accelerate progress towards equal participations- right now.

Methodology of study:

The present paper is mainly based on secondary data. The information has to be collected by us from books, publish data of World Bank report and research papers and journals that provides an entire scenario about women as decision-making leader.

Conclusion:

Women are known to be the symbol of spirituality, strength, love, sacrifice and courage. The role of women in today's world is changing significantly. Women are now well educated and self dependent. They have become successful in many fields like, politics, sports, education, technology, entertainment etc. Today's progressing world has brought a new hope and has empowered women positively. Earlier women were dependent on father or husband, but now they have become capable enough to earn their living. Mother Teresa Kalpana Chawla, Pratibha Patil, Indra Nooyi, P.V Sindhu and many more have become successful in their fields. They are idol for youth across the world. The role of women in today's society is really important. They are working efficiently in all the fields. From housewives, managers to CEO's women are doing their jobs with perfection. Today's women handle the office and home too. Many women are more successful than their male colleagues. They are working at senior leadership level in an excellent way. Women are equally important in the society. Today's women are contributing equally well in country's development and progress. To conclude, women should be encouraged to learn new things and do something apart from the household works. They should be given equal opportunities in all fields. They should be given freedom of choosing their career and making their decision in life.

Reference:

1. A. Remi, (2017), "Women in Leadership and Decision-Making: Understanding Different Style of Leading", Management studies, Vol. 5, No. 6 pp 598-605.

2. M. Diana, T. Gayane, (2020), "Gender Differences in decision0making and Leadership: Evidence from Armenia", Business Ethics and Leadership, Vol. 4, Issue-1, ISSN (Print), pp 2520-6761.

3. D. pilar, H. Rebecca, o. tam, B. Kate, 92015), "Women's Voice and Leadership in Decision-making: Assessing the evidence", ResearchGet.

4. C. Dini, Sowiyah, W. Tri Estu, O.E. Elvira, (2020), "Leadership of Women In Decision Making (Case study In State Islamic, Religious Institute Metro Province Lampung), international Journal of Research and Innovation in Social Science, Vol. iv, Issue. Ix, ISSN 2454-6186.

5. S.R. Bala, Irudyaraj, S George S.J., (2016), "Women Leadership in Organization", Vol. 8, Issue- 2.

6. A. Kaniati, K. Aan, S. Sumarto, H.A. Kholifatul, (2019), " Leadership in Education: Decision-Making in Education", Advances in Social science, Education and Humanities Research, Volume 400.

7. G.T. Nuri, D. Ahmet, B. Taylan, (2021)," Decision- making, Leadership and performance links in private education institutes,", Rajagiri management journal ISSN: 0972-9968.

CHAPTER SEVEN

Challenges in Teaching-Learning before the Teacher Education Programme today

Smt. Madhurima Chaudhuri (Majumder): Assistant Professor, Bhavan's Tripura College of Teacher Education, Narsingarh, Agartala, Tripura (W).

Abstract:

"Education imparted by heart can bring revolution in the society"- said by Maulana Abul kalam Azad. According to Aristotle, "Education is the process of training man to fulfil his aim by exercising all the faculties to the fullest extent as a member of society". Education is a life-long process. It helps people to learn right actions at right time. Teacher performs most crucial role in the field of education to develop an individual to the level of perfection by drawing out the best citizen from him. A teacher is at the center of the teaching-learning process. The importance of teachers can never be underestimated as the future of the students fully depends upon the teachers. The quality of a nation depends upon the quality of its citizens. The quality of citizens depends not exclusively, but in critical measure upon the quality of their education, the quality of their education depends more than upon any single factor, upon the quality of their teacher. So, the quality of teacher education program must be upgraded for producing qualified, efficient and technically skilled teachers. Previously classroom teaching was confined merely with the books and only limited number of teaching aids like black-board, map, chart, globe etc. The teaching was more theoretical in nature. But now with the advancement of Information and Communication technology (ICT), multimedia teaching aids were developed which have not only accelerated the teaching learning process but also made it more dynamic, attractive and interesting. In NEP 2020, Four years integrated teacher education programme (ITEP) is mentioned. A new and National Curriculum Framework for Teacher Education (NCFTE) would be prepared by the NCTE for educating and preparing prospective teachers according to the necessity of the present-day effective education system in India. The new policy promotes online education as a consequence of the Covid-19 pandemic, aiming to make certain readiness with different modes to facilitate learning.

This paper highlighted the different issues and challenges of teacher education and some measures to be taken to resolve these problems. It is very essential to acquire an understanding of the problems and then measures to be formulated to bring about the solutions to the problems.

Key words: Issues, Challenges, Teacher Education, NEP 2020, ITEP, NCFTE, Efficient, Measures.

Introduction: On 29th July, 2020, India got its 3rd National Policy on Education. The Previous two policies were implemented in 1968 and 1986 respectively. This new policy aims to transform India into a knowledge society by making both schools and higher education Institutions more holistic, flexible and multidisciplinary. This new policy is expected to bring a significant change in education system of the country. The policy is a comprehensive frame work for elementary education to higher education as well as vocational training in both rural and urban area of the society.

In the antient time, Education system was teacher centric. The teacher played the principal role. But today, the learner occupies the Centre. Their needs, interests, age, understanding level and potentials are taken into account at first. Nowadays the education is not the process of inputting something to the head, but drawing out from the child. Teachers assess the nature of the students, observe their natural interests, encourage their potential and inspire them to bring out their level best.

We know that teacher is the nation builder. To be able to discharge such a high responsibility, it is very essential that the teacher must become conscious about his role towards the society.

Teacher Education refers to the policies and procedures designed to equip prospective teachers with the pedagogical knowledge, attitude, behaviour and skills they require to perform their tasks effectively in class rooms, schools and outside the four walls. It is a programme which is related to the development of teacher proficiency and competence that would enable and empower the teacher to meet the requirements of the profession and face the challenges therein.

According to the Goods Dictionary of Education, Teacher Education means, - all the formal and non-formal activities and experiences that help to qualify a person to assume responsibilities of a member of the educational profession or to discharge his responsibilities more effectively.

According to the new policy, the education system has to be transformed by 2030. Teacher Education colleges will be converted into multidisciplinary colleges within this time. The students who are interested to be a teacher, for them there will be four years integrated B. Ed course in their under graduate level. They will complete their degree as B.A.(B.Ed.) or B.Sc. (B.Ed.) within this stipulated time. As per NEP 2020 there will not be any substandard stand-alone Teacher Education college in the country.

Major Issues and Challenges in Teacher Education:

Some of the major problems related to teacher education are as under:

- **Problem of Monitoring the Teacher Education Institutions**: The duty of the National Council for Teacher Education (NCTE) is to control the functioning of these Institutions and prevent them from becoming the commercial organization. But it is very difficult on the part of inspection team to visit and monitor so many institutions situated in different parts of the country.

- **Irregularities in selection procedure**:

Selection procedure for admission in teacher education courses should be under strict supervision of governing body, that is NCTE. There should not be any management quota for admission in any institution. A good selection process would not only improve the quality of teacher education course but also provide a suitable candidate for this noble profession.

- **Defective Curriculum**: Curriculum of teacher education in India has been criticized much. The curriculum is rigid and traditional. It is more theoretical and less importance is given to the practical aspects. According to some Educationists, it does not fully address the need of contemporary Indian schools and society. The content must have direct implications in the daily school teaching.

- **Poor academic background of the teacher- trainee**:

Most of the students do not have the requisite academic qualification for entering into the teaching profession. Because of their poor mental ability, after taking admission, they show poor performance.

- **Lack of Subject Knowledge:**

The teacher training programme does not give any importance to the knowledge of basic subjects. The whole practice remains indifferent with regard to the subject knowledge of the teacher-trainee.

- **Lack of proper facilities:**

Large number of institutions have poor financial conditions. They don't have basic facilities such as experimental schools, libraries, laboratories, hostel and college building.

- **Classroom challenges:**

Some of the challenges faced by the teachers include lack of team work, irregularity in student's attendance, working towards long term goals, arguments and excuses.

- **Lack of ICT facilities:**

The main challenges in using ICTs in education is bridging the gap between those who have access to technology and those who do not have. The failure to meet the challenge would mean a further widening of the gap.

- **Lack of co-curricular activities:**

The co-curricular activities in teacher education are unplanned and not sufficient. Due to lack of time these activities are ignored. But nowadays these are very essential in school education.

- **Globalization and Erosion of values:**

Due to globalization and advancement of ICT, world has become closer. Access to all kind of information is very easy. But there are several deviations particularly of young generations who are prone to malpractices. Mobile culture, internet, face book, twitter etc. have polluted the young minds.

Some Other problems of Teacher Education:

- Lack of dedication of the Teacher-trainees towards their professional career.
- Negative attitude of management towards the development of Human resources and material resources.
- Senior secondary level is not included in teacher education.
- Teaching method is not up to the standard.

Measures to be taken to improve the Teacher Education programme:

- Socio-economic status of the teachers must be up graded to attract the talented people towards this profession.
- The teacher education programme should be modified. New and innovative techniques can be used for transaction of curriculum.
- Teacher should be able to think critically, make right decisions and maintain good and harmonious relationship with others.
- Technique used in teaching should develop habit of self-learning and reduce dependence of teachers. Teacher should encourage the students to construct knowledge themselves.
- The evaluation system can be reformed and it can be made reliable, objective, comprehensive and continuous.
- Scientific attitude should be developed and its application for the solution of problems should be encouraged.
- The teacher should have ability to plan and organize the contents of a lesson.
- The teacher should have capacity to find out individual needs of students and to adjust teaching procedures accordingly.
- He/she should have ability to develop and use instructional materials and audio-visual aids.
- The teacher should have the ability to organize, supervise and participate in co-curricular activities of the school.
- He/she should have to help affectively in the guidance programme of the school.

- The teacher should have the knowledge of using ICTs so that they can teach the students in virtual mode as and when necessary.
- Using ICT teacher may share learning resources to the students and provide expert opinion.
- Online teaching-learning method should be implemented as it provides the liberty to learn anything, anytime and anywhere.
- ICT must be used as it shifts teacher centered education into learner centred education, which paves the way to individualized learning.

Conclusion:

One of the potential challenges of teacher education is preparing teachers to facilitate learning among school children. Substantial efforts should be made in curricular practices for preparing teachers in using participatory teaching-learning method, using multiple resources for learning, adopting collaborative learning and executing self-evaluation. Adequate hands-on experience needs to be provided to transform teachers as facilitators in the process of teaching-learning. As there is a rapid shift from behaviourist to constructivist paradigm, there is a need to sensitize teachers to act as a facilitator in allowing school children to construct knowledge.

References:

- National Policy on Education (2020). New Delhi: Government of India (Department of Education).
- Mehrotra, R.N. (1979). "Teacher education: A trend report". In M.B. Buch (Ed.), Second survey of research in education (pp. 414-453). Baroda: Society for Educational Research and Development.
- Sharma, G (2012). 'ICTs' in Teacher Education, Review of Research, 1, 10, 1-4, July.
- Vashist S.R. (2003). Professional Education of Teachers. Jaipur: Mangal Deep.
- www.google.com
- Agarwal, J. C (reprint 2004): Theory and Principles of Education (Philosophical and Sociological bases of Education); Vikash Publishing House Pvt. Ltd. New Delhi.

CHAPTER EIGHT

Issues and Strategies to Improve Women's Empowerment in India

Trisha Paul: Research Scholar, Mahatma Gandhi University, 13th Mile, G.S. Road, Khanapara, Dist-Ri-Bhoi, Meghalaya, trisha28paul@gmail.com, 9051084797/ 8637010563

Abstract

We are living in the 21st century. But gender discrimination, gender bias, gender stereotype, etc. still exist in our modern society. Girls are the prime victims of these problems. Very often girls are deprived even of their fundamental rights. The worst-case scenario is when girls are deprived of their education and get married before completing the age of 18. Girls are deprived due to the lack of awareness and education among family members, prejudices, traditional thinking etc. of society.

For a developing country like India, a girl child is as important as a male child. A country cannot prosper if 50% of its population is lack behind. In a developed country a girl enjoys her full freedom and contributes to developing the country. India is the 5th largest economy in the world and it has the potential to reach the 4th place by 2027. It is not possible without empowering women. It is not true that women are not empowered in India. Women are giving a tough fight in every field to boys. But, some issues regarding women's empowerment exist in our society.

In this study, I would like to discuss the need for women's empowerment. I would also like to discuss the issues we are facing to implement women's empowerment properly. In the end, some important strategies will be discussed as suggestions to improve the condition of women empowerment.

Introduction:

"All nations attain greatness by paying proper respect to women. That country and that nation which does not respect women, has never become great nor will ever be in future. There is no hope of rise for that country or family where women live in sadness"- Swami Vivekananda. According to him, the well-being of the country will not be possible unless women's conditions are improved. He wanted all women to receive adequate education and training so they could contribute to the country's economic, social, and educational reforms. To function effectively in society, they should become leaders and be placed in higher positions.

Objectives:

1. To study the need for women's empowerment
2. To study the issues in women's empowerment
3. To study the strategies to improve women's empowerment

Need for Women's empowerment:

- To stop **child marriage**, it is important that women are empowered. Child marriage is a burning problem in Indian society. Although people are more aware of child marriage nowadays; however, it still exists in many areas of the country.
- The **Dowry system** is one of the problems that we Indians are trying to fight for a long time in Indian society. Although there are laws to fight against it, it is seen many times that brides' fathers are giving dowry willingly, even though they are very poor.
- **Female infanticide** is a problem in our society. Infants are killed in their mother's wombs if they are found as females. It happens due to the poor mentality of a society that girls will go to others' houses after marriage.
- As the fifth largest economy, India cannot effort not to empower women, if it wants to be the third-largest economy by 2030.
- There were 4,28,278 cases of **crimes against women** registered across India in 2021, a 15.3% increase from the previous year. According to NCRB (National Crime Records Bureau) report, it was found that 31.8% of cases were committed by husbands or relatives who were cruel to women, followed by assaults on women with the intent to outrage their modesty (20.8%), kidnappings and abductions of women (17.6%), and

rapes (7.4%) by women. To stop such incidents, women's empowerment is very crucial.

- Women empowerment is also required to bring poverty down in India. Women can also contribute to family building.

Issues in Women's empowerment:

- **Conservatism:** Many Indian still feel that educating girl children is a waste of money as they go to their father-in-law's house after marriage. If girls do not get proper education, it will become a barrier in front of their carrier.
- **Poverty:** India is still fighting against poverty. If there are many children in a family, many parents think that educating boys is a better option than girls as boys will take care of the parents in future.
- **Unsuitable Curriculum:** Demands of the Society for girls and boys are different. But boys and girls have *the* same curriculum at every stage of education.
- **Lack of transport in rural areas:** Transport in many areas of rural India is still very poor. There are many areas where you can not get any transport after sunset.
- **Lack of security:** News of rape, molestation, and kidnapping are very common whenever we turn on the T.V. As a result, parents become anxious to send their daughters far away from their house for a job.
- **One child policy:** Although there is no such law in India yet, still it is seen that many parents want only one child. Parents having only one child often do not want to send their children far away from them for education or jobs.

Strategies to improve Women's empowerment:

- **Awareness program:** Awareness is the most important solution for any kind of problem. Through awareness, we can understand the whole thing from talk to bottom. So, the government, educational institutions, and NGOs can organise awareness programs to make people understand this fact better.
- **Women's scholarship:** We found that poverty is one of the important issues for women's empowerment. So, from the very beginning of the study, if we facilitate them different types of scholarship, it will be very

helpful for them to study and it will also help their family. Therefore, parents will not be very interested in child marriage and will not stop their girl child's education.

- **Women reservation:** Scholarship will help to continue the study of a girl child and after study, if we can able to provide suitable jobs and promote them to give them proper opportunities to get a job, it will definitely be very helpful for women's empowerment.
- **Increase women's engagement:** Previously we discussed women's reservations but this is not enough. Related to the same, if we are able to increase the engagement of women in decision-making in the home, Political issues, educational issues, social issues, games and sports, art and culture etc. So that they can do possible help to identify women's necessities and problems.
- **Construct new strict rules and regulations:** We have so many rules to protect women or save girl-child but that is not enough. Because we are seeing day by day that women harassment, rape etc are not decreasing. So, the government should need to take strict action and introduce new rules.
- **Ground-level monitoring system:** Government should create an account-level monitoring system with the help of local police, NGOs, panchayat or municipality school college etc. So, they can stop and do very immediate action on any woman-related issues.
- **Set age parameter for women:** We all know our government has already set an age for marriage which is 18 years for a girl child. But generally, within 18 years a girl child never completes her study properly and without higher study girl students can never get a good job. The reservation system will not help them in this regard if they get married in child age and stopped their study. So, the minimum age limit should be increased and do mandatory for all. If women are older by their age, they will more mature and will be able to raise their voices against any wrong activity.
- **Social approach:** In this world, each and every society has its own beliefs. If a society is very rigid about women, female children face many issues due to the mentality of the society and its people. If she does not grow comfortably within her own society, how her all-round development is possible? Social support is very important and most needed for every child.

- **Family support:** We have so many examples where society, people, religion etc create so many difficulties but it cannot stop the girls to progress. They create a milestone in their own field. In that case, we will find in most of the cases that they were supported by their families.
- **Adult Education:** Although, there is scope for adult education in our country. But we see people especially those living in rural areas, are not literate. If people are educated, they will realise the importance of education better.
- **Moral development:** We all know that education helps us to develop holistically. Although we often notice that brides are tortured by their well-educated in-laws' families. This is just one example, there are so many incidents happening on a daily basis. In our curriculum, we found moral education is in hidden form. So, teachers should give students lessons about values, so that students developed morality in themselves.
- **Value education:** Value education is recognised as a very important subject in the present context. In India, the importance of value education in the curriculum is also growing rapidly. Value education makes ability in us to judge the differences between right and wrong. So, in this way, value education teaches us to pay the value to the dignified person or the right thing, without any gender biasness. If we have value education, we never disrespect a woman for her gender.
- **Healthy relationship:** Already we have discussed previously how families' positivity plays a vital role in women's empowerment. But in a family, if the mother or any other female member is treated with less value or harassed, children will also use to it. We always teach our children to respect and care about our father and mother equally. If we do the same for others, our next generation will hopefully maintain the same.

Conclusion:

The development of a country is dependent on its population and this population is made of men and women both. So, women's contribution is truly needed for the development of a nation. Of course, we have discussed so many issues of women's empowerment at the start but we always teach our children that each and everyone is the same. Only females and males have some special differences biologically from each other, otherwise, they have the same rights and when we really maintain it and realise it there is no more special need for women's empowerment because, we all are empowered by our own strength and the Almighty.

References

- Crimes Against Women In India Rose 15% In 2021, Delhi Women Panel Asks Governments To Ensure Women's Safety. (2022, August 30). Retrieved October 4, 2022, from https://www.outlookindia.com/

India overtakes UK as the world's fifth-largest economy | World Economic Forum. (n.d.). Retrieved October 21, 2022, from World Economic Forum website: https://www.weforum.org/agenda/2022/09/india-uk-fifth-largest-economy-world/#:~:text=Just%20a%20decade%20ago%2C%20Indian,from%20the%20International%20Monetary%20Fund.

- Ravi, S. (2016). *A COMPREHENSIVE STUDY OF EDUCATION, SECOND EDITION* (pp. 240–259). PHI Learning Pvt. Ltd.

CHAPTER NINE

Importance of Women as Social and Political Leadership

Manoj Das: Ex-student, Department of Education, of "Burdwan University "Rajbati, west Bengal 713104 Mob -9163764375 ,Email Id-das7075@gmail.com

Abstract

Leadership is a process by which an executive can direct, guide and influence the behavior and work of others towards accomplishment of specific goals in a given situation. Leadership is the ability of a manager to induce the subordinates to work with confidence and zeal. The present paper is mainly based on secondary sources of data. The secondary data is also collected from various reference books, national & international research journal, magazine annual reports, and reports in Government, news paper & internet websites that helps in the importance of women as social and political leadership. If the education system can be given a beauty structure to get out of all these problems then the boys and girls will be educated in education along with the boys and the girls will be able to stand on their merits as ideal citizens in society. Being a girl, she will never feel weak. And thinking of himself as a leader, he will shoulder the responsibility of the society, show everyone the right path, and help them to reach their own goals.

Keywords: Honesty, Leadership, Mindfulness, Political , Progressiveness , Women,

Introduction

Women in positions of power are women who hold an occupation that gives them great authority, influence, and/or responsibility in government or in businesses. Historically, power has been distributed among the sexes disparately. Power and powerful positions have most often been associated with men as opposed to women. As gender equality increases, women hold more and more powerful positions in different sectors of human endeavors.

Accurate and proportional representation of women in social systems has been shown to be important to the long-lasting success of the human race and existence. Additionally, a study shows that "absence is not merely a sign of disadvantage and disenfranchisement, but the exclusion of women from positions of power also compounds gender stereotypes and retards the pace of equalization or being equalized."

Concept of Leadership

Leadership is a process by which an executive can direct, guide and influence the behavior and work of others towards accomplishment of specific goals in a given situation. Leadership is the ability of a manager to induce the subordinates to work with confidence and zeal.

Leadership is the potential to influence behavior of others. It is also defined as the capacity to influence a group towards the realization of a goal. Leaders are required to develop future visions, and to motivate the organizational members to want to achieve the visions.

According to Keith Davis, "Leadership is the ability to persuade others to seek defined objectives enthusiastically. It is the human factor which binds a group together and motivates it towards goals."

Objective of the study

- To study the characteristics of leadership in society
- To understand advantage of women leadership in society.
- To find out main obstacle of advancement of women's education in India.
- To identify the measures to improve women education.
- To study the role of education to made good women leader.
- To study importance of women as social and political leadership.

Methodlgy of the study

The present paper is mainly based on secondary sources of data. The secondary data is also collected from various reference books, national & international research journal, magazine annual reports, and reports in Government, news paper & internet websites that helps in the importance of women as social and political leadership.

Characteristics of leadership

• Excellent communication and leadership are all about involving others at various levels. Connecting is the ability to identify with people and communicate with them.

• For group members to be completely self-confident in their leader, they have to trust the leader is a person of truthfulness and reliable character. Honesty is powerfully tied to values and moral principles.

• Leaders frequently bind themselves up in knots wanting every decision to be wonderful, however, the great leaders make decisions they recognize could be incorrect. The actual differentiator is deciding with pace and sincerity.

• Good thinkers explain problems and never lack thoughts to construct their team or their organization. To motivate fresh and innovative thoughts, use time reading books, listening to podcasts, and discussing with innovative thinkers.

• The most efficient leaders remain optimistic and inspirational. People anticipate their leaders to be energized and passionate about their potential. They want to motivate team members with endeavor and a strong belief in where the organization is direction.

• The actual subject is how we handle the confrontment that matters. An efficient leader conducts and resolves conflicts to produce optimal outcomes. The leader understands and effectively applies the skill of shrewdness in the place of work.

• Great team building begins with construction unity, which starts with the leader. To rally a team around a common reason or vision, the leader has to see the vision and continuously keep the team focused on it.

Advantage of women leadership in society

• Family as the fundamental social institution has a thoughtful impression on individuals. As the place of the very first incorporation of individuals into social life, families are the chief resource of their members' necessary personal and social identity and the ability for love and togetherness. An inspiring family is a great enabler for women's leadership. An individual's physical, emotional and psychological development takes shape first in his/her family unit. An individual is what a family creates him/her.

• Women as such represent unity and cooperation. They are essential to the survival of a family – an indispensable social organization. This value of unifying varied minds in a family is an essential characteristic of victorious leadership. An accurate leader acts as a unifying strength to attach the team or the group of followers together and significantly leads them to accomplish the goal. Women acquire such quality considerably and this prepares them eminent leaders.

- Women charge gloriously when it comes to communication at the personal level. They are fairly skillful at communicating with others and score more advanced than men on this front. The ability to converse with people is an essential need to become a significant leader. Women acquire this skill naturally.

- Women be liable to be better listeners than men and this makes them effective communicators. good quality communicators are outstanding listeners. Effectual communication skills start with listening. Women are reasonably better at both listening and communicating.

- Accountability is also a considerable leadership quality. Women rarely pay any attention to their accounts on any issue. It is seen that women are more accountable than men. Accountability may not help in motivating others but is highly radiating.

- A leader who comprehends the value of accountability never puts the responsibility for any loss or mistake on the individual members of a team. The leader rather shoulders the responsibility. It motivates the team members to take charge of any assignment without any repentance or fear.

- Women leaders have the capability to work together with colleagues, clients, and employees across teams, functions, and departments because being mutual is innate to them. Many studies have arranged that women are more cooperative than men.

Main obstacles of advancement of women's education in India

The current rate of progress in women's education in India is not very promising. There are various problems hindering the rapid expansion of women's education. These are the problems.

• A large part of India's population lives in rural areas. Generally, the rural farmers and underdeveloped communities are not at all aware of the need for women's education. Moreover, the girls of these families are married off at a very young age. As a result, they do not get any opportunity to learn.

• Girls have difficulty commuting to school as schools in rural areas are far away.

• From a very early age, rural girls have to help their mothers with household chores in various ways – as a result, they do not have much opportunity to study.

• Boys are more valuable than girls in the eyes of most parents in our country. Therefore, especially in rural areas, parents are not as enthusiastic about teaching boys as they are about teaching girls.

• Various prejudices and conservative attitudes in the Muslim and tribal communities create obstacles to the education of girls.

• Child marriage is still prevalent in underdeveloped communities in India. After marriage, girls do not get special opportunities to study at their in-law's house. Moreover, they become mothers at a young age, so raising children becomes their main task.

• Maternal illiteracy, poverty, and lack of necessary government and public initiatives have also created particular obstacles to the rapid expansion of women's education.

The measures to improve Women's Education

The following measures can be adopted to solve the above problems.

• Arrangements should be made to establish equal status for men and women in society. Employment opportunities for women should be increased so that women can be economically self-reliant.

• Rural farmers and people from underdeveloped communities should be made aware of the need for female education. Prejudices and conservative attitudes among these people must be removed through the promotion of adult education.

• Child marriage should not only be prohibited by law. The illiterate masses should be made aware of the evils of child marriage.

• Arrangements should be made to open more girls' schools to facilitate the education of rural girls. Also, parents should be made aware so that they are interested in girls' education.

• Measures should be taken to eradicate poverty and improve the quality of life of poor people. As a result, children from poor families do not have to earn money as child laborers and instead, governments and welfare institutions have to make special efforts to attract them to schools.

• Mid-day meal should be arranged in the school. If the children of poor families do not get enough to eat for two days, if they get a mid-day meal at school, then the school attendance rate will naturally increase and their path to education will also be smooth.

• Special measures should be taken to remove prejudice and conservative attitudes from the mind of the Muslim and tribal communities.

• Finally, the government and the public must be taken special initiatives to promote women's education.

Role of education to made good women leader

•Education helps women acquire knowledge, understand gender relations, develop a sense of self-worth, a belief in their ability, etc. It enables them to bring out the best in them and make them accepted as a mass leader.

•Education enables women to free themselves from the bondage of ignorance and orthodox beliefs, social evils, gender discrimination, and domestic as well as social violence.

•It creates in them fortitude and self-confidence to fight against every odd on their way to achieving success in life.

•It enlightens them about the larger world and world views. It also acquaints them with women leaders of different countries and their leadership styles. It exposes them to the world and helps them know the conditions of women in different countries and different societies.

Importance of women as social and political leadership

Having women leadership in any association conduct to an additional encouraging environment all around. Women may not always comprehend how collected for the accomplishment they are in leadership roles, but their potential and capabilities are irrefragable.

Sympathy, progressiveness, mindfulness, pressure handling, multitasking, and open communication are some of the natural traits of women leaders which build them additionally in sync with their squad.

Today, many businesses and industries are realizing that women in leadership not only bring significant benefits but are also unrepeatable in the office, boardroom, and at the head of the table.

• The gender pay gap is an occurrence that has persisted in organizations and places of work in spite of decades of development. It has been a long time since organizations have been judged as a way to close this gender pay gap. One promising solution is to offer women leadership in organizations. The gender pay gap is more like a gender chance gap. It has been seen that when males and females start their progress from scratch, men are usually offered more opportunities leading to higher-paying leadership positions. To combat this problem, it is recommended that women should be offered leadership positions. This can help close the pay gap more efficiently.

• Varied experiences and perspectives contribute significantly to bringing innovation as different perspectives lead to better decisions making. Therefore organizations with advanced levels of diversities typically tend to outgrow those with smaller amount variety percentages.

• When women grow to be leaders, they bring skills, diverse perspectives, and structural and cultural dissimilarity which consummately dive into effective solutions to the companies engaged by men. With different perspectives and a sense of awareness, women can explore finer details to see what is actually going on beneath.

• The additional varied a place of work is, the more diverse thoughts move together, thus fueling growth and supporting the sustainability of any association. Diversity in the place of work is not only a substance of men vs. women in leadership roles. It is a topic of having an amalgamation together throughout the whole organization. Workplace gender variant should be the goal of each corporation. It enhancement productivity, and creativity, improves performance, and staff maintenance, and enhances cooperation.

• The authority of position models cannot be refused. Regardless of gender, all people need good mentors who can assist them in developing in their profession. In the ground of counseling and guiding young employees, women leaders are recognized to be a better consultant as compared to men.

• Having women on top of the team can get better processes and improve cooperation. Similarly, groups with more women are enhanced at taking turns in conversations, thus building the most out of groups' information and skill. In businesses and organizations, it has been seen that women are more effective at negotiating and making deals, even when the stakes are high. They can accomplish understanding and create deals where men go down short, but first, they must be known for leadership and authoritative positions.

Conclusion

Based on the above discussion we can conclude that half of the world's work is done by men and women. In the patriarchal society of the past, males engaged themselves in the work of the society as leaders but in those days girls were not allowed to go out of the house. Studies were conducted according to male norms. Education was not freedom; it was their world to raise their family and children. As the education system improved with the speed of time, importance was given to the education of boys as well as girls. According to the constitution, boys and girls are given equal rights to education in all fields. Till now there are various obstacles in the education sector, such as lack of education in rural areas, lack of quality teachers, lack of finance, and a stagnant state of management. If the education system can be given a beauty structure to get out of all these problems then the boys and girls will be educated in education along with the boys and the girls will be able to stand on their merits as ideal citizens in society. Being a girl, she will never feel weak. And thinking of himself as a leader, he will shoulder the responsibility of the society, show everyone the right path, and help them to reach their own goals.

References

1) https://www.linkedin.com

2) https://www.peterlang.com

3) https://www.amacad.org

4) https://www.iss.edu.

5) https://www.triplepundit.com

6) https://www.tutorialspoint.com/women_in_leadership

7) https://womendeliver.org/womensleadership

8) Rey . de . la C . (2005) "Gender , women and leadership " Agenda empowering women for gender equity No . 65 , women and leadership (2005) , PP, 4-11 (8pages) Published by : Taylor & Francis , Ltd . https://www.jstor.org/stable/4066646

9) Ziegler . A .(2022) "The Importance of Women Leadership" https://community.themomproject.com

10) https://www.managementstudyguide.com/women-and-leadership.

CHAPTER TEN

Mental Health Problems of Female Sex Workers in India

Nairika Dhar: Research Scholar, Education, mailmenairika@gmail.com

Introduction

The concept of mental health is as old as human evolution. A mentally healthy person is one, who has a balanced personality, free from schism and inconsistencies, emotional and nervous tensions, discords and conflicts, a well adjusted person can deal with his potentialities as well as he can accept his limitations. Now a days mental health problems are a significant cause of the global burden of diseases which can affect persons' personality, thought processes or social interactions. Mental health issues can often be difficult to clearly diagnose, unlike physical illnesses. According to the World Health Organisation (WHO), India's mental health workforce is severely understaffed. The National Mental Health Survey 2016 found that close to 14 per cent of India's population required active mental health interventions. Every year, about 2,00,000 Indians take their lives. Roughly 56 million Indians suffer from depression, and 38 million suffer from some anxiety disorder. An analysis based on gender revealed that women are more prone to suffer from mental health issues than men. Around 3.8 per cent of men and 3 per cent of women faced anxiety disorders due to bullying and victimisation. Unfortunately, 5 percent of men and about 8.3 percent women were vulnerable to childhood sexual-abuse.

A sex worker is a person who provides <u>sex work</u>, either on a regular or occasional basis. The term "sex worker" was coined in 1978 by sex worker activist <u>Carol Leigh</u>. The term is used in reference to those who work in all areas of the <u>sex industry</u>. Female sex workers (FSWs) face intersecting socio-economic and structural inequalities starting in early childhood that may increase their risk of mental health problems across their life course.

These inequalities include poverty, low education, childhood neglect and violence, gender inequality, police arrest, alcohol and substance use, discrimination, violence from clients and intimate partners and high prevalence of Human Immunodeficiency Virus (HIV)/Sexually Transmitted Infections (STIs). As female sex workers (FSWs) are at increased risk of mental health problems, including mood disorders and substance abuse, it is needed to understand the origins of these mental health issues for proper intervention and prevention. Along this it is necessary to identify how the context in which they sell sex impacts their mental health. The negative societal attitude of sex work and their psycho-social challenges force sex workers to conceal aspects of their identity and this leads to low self-esteem and self-worth. Many sex workers do not disclose their occupation to family and friends, which in turn makes them socially isolated. Social isolation then makes them mentally disturbed. Specific mental health disorders that are prevalent in the sex-worker population are anxiety disorders, post-traumatic stress disorder, mood disorders and substance abuse.

Prevalence of Mental Health problems of female sex workers

FSWs have been found to be at higher risk for mental health disorders, including depression, anxiety, social stigma etc. Consequently, FSWs suffering from mental health disorders might be at an increased risk of engaging in unsafe behaviour such as unprotected sex or substance use. As a result they may thus be at higher risk in accusing HIV infection as well as would face higher degree of challenges in accessing care or support services due to their stigmatized and marginalized status. Moreover, FSWs are the commonest victim of violence, abuse and social discriminatory practices. All these underlying factors act as barriers in accessing treatment and other support services. Therefore depression may have a farfetched implication in sex workers life and could adversely affect the well-being of FSWs. Many studies have shown that depression is significantly associated with the high risk of becoming HIV infected. Sex workers in India are especially at higher risk of suffering from depression due to the constellation of cultural challenges that they face. The situation is aggravated by the stigma attached to mental health including social isolation which is often confronted by individuals suffering from depression. However, there is very little scholarship on depression with specific focus to sex workers in India, and its association with the elevated levels of HIV risk. Moreover, there is no specific strategy and intent to initiate mental health interventions for sex workers to address depression including its association with HIV risk taking behaviour. Various studies conducted worldwide indicate that female commercial sex workers (FCSWs) have higher rates of psychiatric problems as well as health-related issues. A study conducted by Deb reveals that the majority of the FSWs had been suffering from depression. Vanwesenbeeck also found that in a sample of 96 sex workers, the prevalence of depression was 73%. Lakshmana *et al.* indicated that a majority (72.9%) of the FSWs were using one or other substances among which alcohol (58.6%) was the most frequently used substance. Pandiyan *et al.* found that anxiety, alcohol abuse and psychological morbidity (depression and adjustment disorder) were present in FSWs. Bhat reported the prevalence of neurotic disorders in commercial sex workers to be 45%, and 94% had depressive disorders.

Factors affecting Mental Health of female sex workers

Sex workers have been struggling with mental health issues for many reasons that can be related to their work, as well as completely separate from it. Recent research conducted specifically with sex workers with mental health issues indicated that large numbers of participants experienced different mental health problems prior to starting sex work. For many of these, sex work was seen as one viable option to gain or seek financial stability, as they faced barriers to obtaining and keeping mainstream work due to their mental health needs (Macioti et al., 20212). However, there are several structural factors particularly affecting the mental health of sex workers. They include stigma, criminalisation (of sex work and migration in particular), poverty, homelessness and poor working conditions. Other factors impacting on sex workers' mental health are violence in and outside work and factors linked to further intersectional marginalisation (e.g. based on gender identity, residence status, sexuality, race, ethnicity, age etc.)

Societal stigma impacts the mental health of sex workers to a very great extent. Concretely, stigma means that many sex workers fear being outed about their work to friends, family members, random people, healthcare professionals, social services, teachers, authorities, work colleagues in other jobs, and so forth. A participant in the focus group indicated that being outed meant losing social status. Sex workers can not be able to lead a normal life due to societal stigma. As a result they suffer from various mental health issues like trauma, low self-esteem, loneliness etc. Social isolation and loneliness strongly impact the mental health of sex workers. On the other hand stigma acts as an umbrella factor that intertwines with many other structural factors influencing the mental health of sex workers, such as criminalisation or violence. Social isolation, stigma and the lack of a supportive legal environment are factors that may increase the risk of violence, which negatively impacts the mental health of sex workers. Outing oneself does not only mean losing social status but can also lead to violence. In many countries, sex workers mostly face violence from the police, as reported by ESWA member and sex worker-led organisation. Sex workers are faced extortion, arbitrary detention, threats and blackmail, humiliation and degrading treatment by the police.

Bad working conditions are another clear factor affecting sex workers mental health (Macioti et al. 2021; Macioti et al. 2017). These include the absence of a safe environment to work, unsupportive or exploitative managers and operators, insecure labour arrangements and the lack of workers' protection and social security. They range from precarious working conditions to exploitation and trafficking experiences, and can strongly affect sex workers' mental health.

Preventive measures of Mental Health issues

Recognising sex work as work through decriminalisation is the first, necessary step towards improving sex workers' mental health. Some community projects and organisations known to or members of ESWA provide support that helps with mental health issues. But first of all, there is an urgent need to secure the environment of female sex workers much more intensively. This could be performed by securing the physical environment as well as by several legal and administrative measures. As the group of sex workers is very heterogeneous, the factors of burden contributing to ill mental health have also to be identified individually and improved. Health professionals need to understand the reasons why women end up in street sex work. Viewing the health problems of female street sex workers in the context of a history of childhood and adult trauma including sexual abuse, abandonment and social exclusion health professionals should become empathetic and take necessary measures for prevention. To meet the needs of disadvantaged groups, which includes female sex workers, health services should develop and implement policies that mitigate social exclusion and discourage social stigma (National Institute for Health and Care Excellence, 2013). In view of the frequent history of childhood trauma and vulnerability of female street sex workers, nurses should take particular care to address safeguarding concerns in both adults and children. Mobile facilities such as condom vans have a valuable role in health promotion and helping to prevent the spread of sexually transmitted diseases, as does providing free condoms. Since the majority of sex workers endure higher levels of violence from police officers, pimps, madams and clients, most of these women are constantly struggling with suicide, sexually transmitted diseases, terminal illnesses, and deep-rooted suffering such as the stability of their own mental health. Shahmanesh et al. (2009) define these injustices as the silent epidemic in India. Stigma and discrimination are prevalent in the health care system. In countries like India, health 26 care facilities are readily available for people. However, if a person is from a marginalized group like sex workers they will most likely be unable to access those health care systems because of the stigma attached to them. The health care system further victimizes sex workers as negative attitudes among healthcare staff prevent sex workers seeking treatment. Fear, anxiety and denial associated with HIV/AIDS can be attributed to traumatic experiences female sex workers have faced within health care facilities. Rennie and Behets (2004) further emphasize that 180 million people will require HIV/AIDS testing every year.

Now a days female sex workers are an extensively marginalised social group, and they are facing many difficult challenges in different spheres of life including economical level, psychological level and social level. All these spheres are interconnected and the effect on one sphere would be affecting the other one. As the female sex workers belong to the disadvantaged group of society it is quite obvious that they would have been deprived from all the facilities. Their health issues are ignored. The lack of professional mental health support and financial support are also identified. Even most of the sex workers are unaware about their mental health issues. Also FSWs are said to be unaware of the need for mental health support. Female sex workers in India require tailor-made action plans and policies to support them including alternative livelihood and financial schemes such as economic schemes, pensions and scholarships for their children. Policymakers and mental health professionals can take necessary measures to develop need-based interventions and to design in-depth research. As we are living in 21st Century we should be progressive enough to make favourable attitude towards the marginalized groups of our society and try to bring them into mainstream life. Given the ever-increasing focus of government, funders, and professionals on including female sex workers in various schemes and programmes, it is imperative to make a distinction between programmes that are for women, and women empowerment.

Because in the present scenario, anything happening with, or for women, falls under the category of 'women empowerment'.

References

1] Beksinska et al. (2021). Prevalence and correlates of common mental health problems and recent suicidal thoughts and behaviours among female sex workers in Nairobi, Kenya. *BMC Psychiatry*, Vol – 21(503), page – 17.

2] Jana S et al. (2017). Depression and Its Relation with HIV Risk and Social Well-Being among the Brothel-Based Female Sex Workers in Kolkata, India. *J Community Med Public Health Care*, Vol – 4(1), page - 12.

3] Kanayama et al. (2022). Mental Health Status of Female Sex Workers Exposed to Violence in Yangon, Myanmar. *Asia Pacific Journal of Public Health*, Vol- 34(4), pp - 354–361.

4] Marboh Goretti Laisuklang and Arif Ali (2017). Psychiatric Morbidity among Female Commercial Sex Workers. *Indian J Psychiatry*, Vol – 59(4), pp – 465-470.

5] Suresh G et al. (2009). An Assessment of the Mental Health of Street-Based Sex Workers in Chennai, India. *Journal of Contemporary Criminal Justice,* Vol – 25(2), pp- 186-201.

6] Tara S H Beattie et al. (2020). Mental health problems among female sex workers in low- And middle-income countries: A systematic review and meta-analysis. Plos Medicine, Vol – 17(9), page –38.

7] V Poliah and S Paruk (2017). Depression, anxiety symptoms and substance use amongst sex workers attending a nongovernmental organisation in KwaZulu-Natal, South Africa. South African Family Practice, Vol – 59(3), pp – 116-122.

8] Zehnder et al. (2019). Stigma as a Barrier to Mental Health Service Use Among Female Sex Workers in Switzerland. *Front. Psychiatry*, Vol – 10.

About The Book

The book *"Women Empowerment and Leadership"* is pertinent to recognize the fact that women play a crucial role in the economic and political development of a nation. Women education in India has been a major concern of the government as well as civil society since educated women can play an important role in the development of the country. Education enables women to respond to the challenges, to confront their traditional role and to change their lives. It strengthens economies and reduces inequality. They earn higher income and participate in decision making which further brings about positive changes in themselves and their families. Hence, it has been an urgent necessity to invest in Women' education, which can transform communities, countries, and the entire world, thereby contributing to more stable, resilient societies that give all people an equal the opportunity to fulfill their full potential.

Editor's Profile

Dr. Savita Mishra is a Principal, Vidyasagar College of Education, Phansidewa, Darjeeling, West Bengal. She has impeccable records of nineteen years of teaching and research activities. She has written more than 150 research articles in reputed National and International journals and authored 70 books. She has also developed a psychological tool for assessing Attitude towards Science. She is the National resource person & Master trainer of MGNCRE, Ministry of Education, Government of India. She has awarded Best Teacher Award 2010 from Sikkim central University, Best Principal award 2020, Best Academician Award 2020, Celebrity writer award 2020, Excellent Achiever award 2020, Women Researcher Award 2021, Best Teacher Award (Higher Education) 2021, India Prime Top 100 Women Icon Award 2021 and Outstanding Scientist Award 2021. She has been conferred the title of 'Leading Educationists of the World' by IBC, Cambridge, London.